He Included Me

He Included Me

The Autobiography of Sarah Rice

Transcribed and Edited by Louise Westling

The University of Georgia Press   Athens and London

© 1989 by the University of Georgia Press
Athens, Georgia 30602
All rights reserved

Designed by Sandra Strother Hudson
Set in Linotron 10½ on 14 Monticello
The paper in this book meets the guidelines for permanence and
durability of the Committee on Production Guidelines for Book
Longevity of the Council on Library Resources.

Printed in the United States of America

93 92 91 90 89   5 4 3 2 1

Library of Congress Cataloging in Publication Data

Rice, Sarah, 1909–
    He included me : the autobiography of Sarah Rice / transcribed and
  edited by Louise Westling.   p. cm.
    ISBN 0-8203-1141-3 (alk. paper)
    1. Rice, Sarah, 1909– . 2. Afro-Americans—Alabama—
Biography.   3. Afro-Americans—Florida—Biography.   4. Alabama—
Biography.   5. Florida—Biography.   6. Afro-Americans—Southern
States—Social life and customs.   7. Southern States—Social life and
customs—1865–   I. Westling, Louise Hutchings.   II. Title.
E185.97.R53A3 1989
975.9'06'0924—dc19
[B]   88-38690
                                                             CIP

British Library Cataloging in Publication Data available

Title page photograph: Sarah with students, early 1930s

Contents

Preface

At the beginning of *Invented Lives*, Mary Helen Washington questions why the traditions of black culture seem to be predominantly masculine and asks, "How does the heroic voice and heroic image of the black woman get suppressed in a culture that depended on her heroism for its survival?" However they may have been suppressed, the voices and images of these black women have begun to emerge in the past decade and to fill out the whole story of the black experience in America. Sarah Lucille Webb Rice is a remarkable woman whose life story is a significant addition to this record.

Born in rural Alabama in 1909, she was the third child of a young schoolteacher named Lizzie Janet Lewis Webb and her husband, Willis James Webb, a minister in the African Methodist Episcopal church. From an early age, she worked with the rest of her family to wrest a living from a small sharecropping farm, raising cotton and corn, field peas, greens, and other garden vegetables on which their survival depended. She went to school as far as it could take a black child in those days, through the ninth grade, and then began teaching in rural Alabama schools herself. She married a handsome farmer and became a mother, but that first marriage did not work out. Then a long span of hard times began with the depression. These took her eventually to Florida, where she had to become a worker in private homes to support herself and her son. Eventually she met and married Andrew A. Rice, a good and devout man who was her companion until his death in 1983. In the years since her move to Jacksonville, Florida, in the late 1930s, she has won a respected place for herself in her community, as a political leader, as a major figure in her church on the statewide level, and as the confidante and wise friend of white employers as well as her own extended family and wide circle of black friends. Her courage, her integrity, her dignity, her generosity, and her robust humor pervade the story she tells of her life.

He Included Me is an oral narrative that is part of a tradition reaching back at least two hundred years in North America. The tradition actually began on another continent, with African storytelling, but was first recorded on our shores in slave narratives told by those who escaped from southern bondage before the Civil War. The most famous of these is of course Frederick Douglass's *Narrative*, and its plot structure is typical in the way it recapitulates the narrator's physical journey up through adversity to freedom and some measure of success. In our own century such leaders as Booker T. Washington (*Up from Slavery*, 1900) and James Weldon Johnson (*Along This Way*, 1934) continued to see their lives in this black Horatio Alger pattern. But these men were unusual among their people in being able to write their stories and have them published commercially. Literacy set them apart from the vast majority of black Americans and involved them in a literary mode dominated by white men and white idioms.

The most vital currents of narrative art in black culture have been oral, and this stream of verbal tradition began to be collected by folklorists, sociologists, and anthropologists during the early decades of the century when black writers like James Weldon Johnson, Jean Toomer, and Langston Hughes were learning to capture their cultural heritage in poetry and fiction. The WPA projects of the 1930s recorded the accounts of former slaves telling their life stories, while at the same time many of the musical forms of black narrative and poetry sung by such folk artists as Robert Johnson and Huddie Ledbetter were being recorded in sound studios. Most of these examples of oral tradition were brief or fragmentary in form, however, and although they preserved valuable cultural materials, they did not include sustained narratives of individual lives.

Then came the social upheavals of World War II and the civil rights movement. In 1969 a Harvard graduate student named Theodore Rosengarten met Ned Cobb, an eighty-four-year-old survivor of twelve years of imprisonment for activities associated with the Alabama Sharecroppers' Union. A collaboration between the two men produced a remarkable oral autobiography that became a model for the newly developing genre of oral history. Rosengarten worked with Ned Cobb for two years, in thirty-one recording sessions adding up to more than one hundred hours of taped stories. He also interviewed other members of Cobb's family. Then he pieced the recorded materials together, arranging them chronologically and editing for clarity and historical interest. The resulting narrative, *All God's Dangers* (1974), spans three generations and, as Rosengarten explains in his preface, provides a black, nonfiction counterpart to William Faulkner's fictional chronicle of white rural life of the same period in the South's social history. Although *All God's Dangers* resulted from an unusual collaboration between an illiterate, rural black storyteller and an educated, urban white listener, it was an enterprise not without precedent. White listeners had also played a role in the production of slave narratives during the abolition movement in the middle of the nineteenth century. Often they wrote down the oral stories of illiterate slaves, but the two most celebrated examples involved escapees who could read and write. William Lloyd Garrison performed a mediating and supporting role in the evolution of Frederick Douglass's autobiography, and Amy Post and Lydia Maria Child encouraged Harriet Jacobs to write and publish *Incidents in the Life of a Slave Girl*.

The differences between these two nineteenth-century narratives and Ned Cobb's autobiography are differences of geography and narrative medium. Douglass and Jacobs fled their native places for freedom in the North, but once transplanted to urban surroundings, they were able to write their own stories. Ned Cobb remained all his life in rural Alabama and never learned to read or write. Though he needed more assistance to get his narrative in print, his illiteracy was a paradoxical advantage in the age of portable recording equipment. Cobb's oral talent was free to express itself authentically, and Rosengarten could use the tape recorder to capture Cobb's exact words and the spoken sound of a lost world.

The autobiographical works I have been describing document the lives of heroic black Americans, but most of them are the stories of men's lives and do not properly acknowledge the role of black women.

Mary Helen Washington points out the notable example of Frederick Douglass's deliberate exclusion from his *Narrative* of the crucial part his future wife, Anna Murray, played in his escape from Baltimore. Not until the feminist movement of the 1960s did the autobiographical narratives of black women begin to take their place in the tradition; indeed, *Incidents in the Life of a Slave Girl* was little known until feminist scholars began to defend its legitimacy and demonstrate its central importance in the 1970s. Black women have been telling their own stories throughout the twentieth century in both fiction and autobiography, but against heavy odds and usually with only intermittent support from publishers and audiences until recent years. Mary Helen Washington testifies to revived interest in these narratives in *Invented Lives*, an anthology and commentary including work by Harriet Jacobs, Frances E. W. Harper, Pauline Hopkins, Zora Neale Hurston, and Gwendolyn Brooks, as well as less well known writers like Marita Bonner, Nella Larson, and Ann Petry. In the years after these women published their narratives, the civil rights movement stimulated a new interest in autobiography. Anne Moody wrote *Coming of Age in Mississippi* (1968) as a personal account of her upbringing and her experiences as a college girl involved in the dramatic events of the movement; Maya Angelou published a series of autobiographical narratives beginning with *I Know Why the Caged Bird Sings* (1970), and Mary Mebane's *Mary* (1981) and its sequel *Mary, Wayfarer* (1983) describe growing up in North Carolina. Toni Morrison and Alice Walker have given fictional form to the lives of black women in such novels as Morrison's *The Bluest Eye* (1970), *Sula* (1973), and *Beloved* (1987), and Walker's *Meridian* (1976) and *The Color Purple* (1982).

But all of these works were written by women who had broken out of the rural life of poverty that most of their sisters endured. There has been a great need to hear the voices of women who are not professional writers or activists. Sarah Rice gives us one of these voices. Together with Sara Brooks's *You May Plow Here*, Sarah Rice's *He Included Me* balances Ned Cobb's picture of rural Alabama life in the early decades of the twentieth century. These two narratives complement each other as oral presentations of women's experiences in that world. Both recapture lost customs and bring memorable people back to life, but Sarah Rice's story remains centered in the South, while Brooks's is the story of a woman who migrated north and spent her adulthood working in private homes in Cleveland, Ohio. Sarah Rice is an unusually articulate person who speaks for millions of southern black women whose lifelong work has never been recognized or described. As a former schoolteacher, she has the educational background that many lack, and yet she also has the experience of hard and ill-paid work, single motherhood, and community life that characterizes so many of her sisters.

Mrs. Rice is a gifted storyteller who, in undertaking this autobiography, knew exactly what she wanted to say. The initiative for the project was hers, in response to the urging of family members and friends that she record the story of her life. Through my sisters and brother in Jacksonville, she let me know that she would like my help. We have known each other for thirty years, ever since she began working for my mother once a week when I was fourteen. In the intervening years, though I grew up and moved to the opposite corner of the country, we have continued the close relationship that is typical of Mrs. Rice's associations with families in which she has worked. Thus when we began the project, we had a rapport which made the collaboration relaxed, even as it must certainly also have limited some elements of the narrative. Control of the narrative's shape and progress was always Mrs. Rice's. My job was simply to turn on the tape recorder and occasionally interject a question for clarification.

The project involved three separate weeks of recording sessions spread out over a year's time. The first of these took place in the spring of 1986, at the dining room table in Mrs. Rice's Jacksonville home. For four full days she gave an almost uninterrupted chronological account of her life—enough to fill ten ninety-minute tapes. I took the tapes back home with me to Oregon and transcribed them over a four-month period. As each transcription was completed, I sent a copy to Mrs. Rice for her editing. Then in August, she came out to Oregon for a week during which we sat at my dining room table and went over the transcriptions, filling in gaps and clearing up confusions. This second week of recording produced four more tapes. Editing of all this material went on for nine months and was followed by a third session of collaboration and recording in June 1987 in Jacksonville. The reading version was finished in late summer. My task as editor consisted primarily of combining the materials from the three recording sessions and rearranging some elements for narrative coherence. Repetitions and passages that represented digressions from Mrs. Rice's own experiences were deleted, but the stories are hers as she told them, and the idiom is always hers. Some minor additions, such as dates or place names, were made in the interest of narrative clarity.

From the beginning it was clear that Sarah Rice's voice and her narrative mode were central to the integrity of her autobiography and had to be preserved. The resulting story of her life therefore lacks some of the factual precision and the explicit and systematic structure that we associate with literary biography, but it has the vividness, warmth, and humor of a strong individual's voice that can only be transmitted orally. *He Included Me* develops anecdotally, in the natural form in which memories are stored in our minds.

There are many descriptions of the physical details of a vanished way of daily life, such as the account of hog butchering in the rural Alabama autumn and the ways older children took care of their infant siblings while their mothers were at work in the fields or in town. Unusual elements in this picture of rural southern life are Mrs. Rice's recollections of interactions between poor whites and their black neighbors and a detailed sense of rural black education in the early decades of the century. Sarah Rice recalls the development of her own life within this context, in a series of dramatic units, each with its distinctive setting, its story's beginning and movement toward climax, and its point or moral. She uses her ear for dialogue, her sense of concrete detail, and her instinct for dramatic timing to shape these episodes with sure focus and immediacy. For instance, a story she tells of sweeping trash on her imposing minister father from the front porch, when he ordered her to come at once to go work in the field, illustrates her strong will and individuality. The title of the autobiography comes from two parallel incidents where first mother and then daughter exercised their ingenuity and their faith in finding food when all resources seemed exhausted, and each incident is a vivid miniature drama illustrating the providence of God in including the family in his care.

Sarah Rice's childhood independence of character and penchant for feisty self-defense evolved into mature dignity under the guidance of firm parents who taught their children to work hard and respect themselves in spite of the poverty and social injustice around them. The resourcefulness she exercised at the age of six in saving herself from punishment at the hands of a school principal expressed itself in later years in the refusal to be bullied by her first two husbands or to be demeaned by white employers. These qualities further developed into a political shrewdness that made her a natural leader in PTA work, in community politics, and in the statewide women's association of her Baptist church.

He Included Me is a unique contribution to the emerging history of black Americans and a vivid work of oral autobiography full of humor and steady courage. I feel privileged to have been involved with its publication.

Louise Westling

Chronology

1900   Elizabeth Janet Lewis marries Willis James Webb in Fort Mitchell, Alabama.

1902   Charity Beatrice Webb born in Greer, Alabama.

1906   Albert Webb born in Hartford, Alabama.
Webb family moves to Enterprise, Alabama, where Rev. Webb and several other AME ministers begin the Coffin County School.

1909   Sarah Lucille Webb born January 4, in Clio, Alabama.

1911   Webb family moves to Troy, Alabama.

1912   Webb family moves to Andalusia, Alabama.
James Webb born.
Late in the year, family moves to Birmingham, Alabama.

1914   Judge David Webb (J.D.) born.

1917   Elizabeth Webb (Lib) born.
Webb family moves to Batesville, Alabama.

1919   Catherine Webb born.

1921   Family moves to Eufala, Alabama.

1923   Freeman Webb born dead.

1924   Frank Tank Webb born.

1925   Willis James Webb dies in his pulpit of heart failure.
Sarah Webb graduates valedictorian from high school, gets private school job at Mount Level Baptist Church.
Mrs. Webb buys a farm with husband's life insurance.

1926   Sarah passes Alabama State Teachers' Exam and is sent to her first public school job in Clio.

1927   Sarah marries Ernest ("Jim") Hayes.
Mrs. Webb marries Elder Dickerson and moves to his farm six miles outside Eufala.

1928   Sarah gives birth to James David Hayes on April 23.

1929   Sarah leaves Jim Hayes and returns to live with her mother.

1929–   Sarah teaches in Rocky Mount, Clayton, Ariton, and
33   Pinkard, Alabama.

1933   Sarah moves to Panama City, Florida, to work for Dr. and Mrs. Wells.

1935   Sarah teaches in Westbay, Florida.

1936   Sarah teaches in Bayou George, Florida.

1937   Sarah moves to Jacksonville, Florida, and marries James Myers.
Sarah begins working for Mrs. Livesey.

1938   Catherine marries David Frost in Eufala.

1939   Sarah moves into a house on Davis Street with Lib and James David.
Sarah begins working for Mrs. Thompson.

1947   Sarah buys a Jim Walter house on Castellano Avenue.

1949   Sarah's mother moves to Jacksonville and builds a house on Castellano.
Lib and J.D. also build in the neighborhood about this time.

1953   Sarah marries Andrew A. Rice in January.

1956   Sarah begins working for Mrs. Hutchings.

1973   Sarah almost dies of carbon monoxide poisoning.

1983   Rice dies of a stroke.

He Included Me

CHAPTER ONE

Early Days in Clio and Birmingham (1909–1917)

M y name is Sarah Rice. I was born in Clio, Alabama, on January 4, 1909. My father, Willis James Webb, was a Methodist minister in the African Methodist Episcopal church, and my mother, Lizzie Janet Lewis Webb, was a teacher. When I was a little girl, Mama would tell us stories of her courtship, how she met Papa, and different things about her sisters and brothers and about working for the doctor and his family who sent her to school, and about my granddaddy, Albert Lewis, who was born during slavery time.

Mama said that my great-grandmother was half white. During that time, the mulattoes were treated better than the regular blacks. They were used for the housework and not put out in the fields as much. So my great-grandmother and her children worked in the big house. I remember Mama telling us about how our great-grandmother had gorgeous hair. During that time the women were wearing their hair in big round curls, ringlets, so she ringletted hers. But her mistress didn't like it and took her and cut it all off. Then her hair just curled and looked pretty cut short that way.

Some of the aristocratic things came down the line with people like my great-grandmother. The fine things of life came to us from them, because they were living in the houses and saw them and acquired manners and good English and an interest in learning, which was good for any generation of people.

When freedom time came, my granddaddy was a young man. He used to drive the buggy for his mistresses, and he would see them drinking water out of a glass. He always had to drink out of a gourd, even at home, and he just wanted some day to be able to drink water out of a glass. It looked so crystalline and so fascinating to him, to see those ladies drinking out of a glass.

Later on, he married and had a family in Fort Mitchell, Alabama. His wife's name was Sarah, or Sallie, and their children were Lizzie (born in 1870), Sis, Cattie, Judge, and Theodore Roosevelt. My granddaddy Lewis was killed in a cotton gin in about 1906.

Sarah Lewis, my grandmama, was a midwife and nursed many of her friends, white and black. She worked with a white doctor out there in the country. He would go among the white people and would always have Sallie come in and help him and see after the people for two weeks or so, kind of nurse them, and then go on to another one. She passed in 1921.

My daddy was born near Cedar Hill, Georgia, May 25, about 1870. He was the baby from his daddy's first marriage, and when his daddy married again after his mama died, his stepmother was mean all the time to him. She had children of her own and was jealous of the previous wife's children. When my daddy was twelve years old, he left home because his stepmother had his daddy to almost kill him for drinking some sweet milk. You weren't supposed to touch that milk until they had taken the butter off and it had turned to clabber and they had made buttermilk. You drank the buttermilk; you didn't drink that sweet milk.

Daddy ran away from home, and he would walk during the nighttime and hide in the bushes during the daytime to keep from being caught by his father. He went to a white lady who was a widow woman and had a farm, and he started working by the month for her. She called him Jimmy, and he stayed in the barn. That lady taught him how to read and write, and he could write beautifully, and was a good reader, and he studied hard. He stayed there and worked until he was about nineteen years old, when he was called into the ministry.

He used to pick a banjo, and he'd play for the white people when they danced. One night he was picking for them, and a revival meeting was happening up the road. He slipped away to the revival and joined the church and started preaching. He preached for about two years until he got discouraged and stopped. Then he got deathly sick with a fever of some kind, didn't know what it was. But he said this lady nursed him. She told him, "Jimmy, don't you think that maybe God is watching you? You said he called you." She said, "I believe that if you prayed and asked Him to forgive you and recommitted yourself to Him, you might get better." By then he was just skin and bones, couldn't eat anything. He did what she said, and he got better. In my presence after I was a big girl, he told us that he had promised God that when he got real sick before he died, he wanted to go back to his church and preach. When that time came, Mama said, "You're not able."

But he said, "I promised God. If I die in the pulpit, it's okay with me." And that's what he did—he went back to his church and preached, and he passed out and died.

My mama's education was different from Papa's. Mama worked for a doctor's wife as the nursemaid for her children. Mama caught on to a lot of their culture; her English was much better than mine. She always had a wonderful imagination. The doctor's wife saw the potential in Mama, and when that lady's children grew up, she told Grandmama, "Lizzie ought to go to school; she's real good." Well, Mama was about sixteen then, and the doctor's wife helped her to go to school in Columbus, Georgia, where she finished the ninth grade. That was a lot back then, and it's what made her a professional. When you finished the ninth grade back then, you were almost equivalent to a first year of college now.

They helped Mama, and she became a teacher. My mama could do so many things—teach and sing and cook out of this world, everything. Looked like she was just artistic, because she could draw and design. When she wanted to make clothes for us, she could look at a dress and make one just like it without a pattern.

After Mama finished school, she met my father in Fort Mitchell, Alabama, at a Sunday school convention where she was a delegate. Two handsome men had been courting her, but then Willis James Webb came along. He was very black and tall and skinny, a preacher. They courted for a year, and then Mama married him in 1900. Because

Papa was preaching in little country churches and was often transferred by the AME Conference from one to the other, they seemed to be moving every year or two, all over Alabama. In 1902, when they were living in Greer, their first child was born, and Papa named her Charity Beatrice for his mother, who had died when he was little.

When Beatrice was a baby, Mama and Papa carried her with them when they went to visit her mother. Grandmama asked where were the baby's clothes. Mama said, "In that sack."

Grandmama looked in there and said, "Is this all the baby's got? You all don't have any more clothes than this?"

Mama said, "We're saving for her education."

Grandmama said, "Well, that's good. How much have you got saved?"

Mama looked at Papa. Not one penny had they saved. They hadn't been able to save a dime. Mama said, "We don't have anything yet." But they did it as time went by. They sent us all to school.

In 1906, when they were living in Hartford, my brother Albert was born. He was named for Papa's mother's father. They were living in the parsonage of Wesley Chapel, where Papa was preaching and Mama was teaching. Mama also washed and ironed for the white minister and his wife and for Mrs. Pinkie Strickland. The preacher was Reverend Ellison, and he was a Methodist. Since Papa was a Methodist preacher too, although he was AME, they had a lot in common and became friends.

About 1906, Papa and Mama moved out from Hartford to Enterprise, Alabama, where he and several other Methodist ministers started a Methodist school named the Coffin County School after their bishop, L. J. Coffin. Papa and Mama mortgaged the land they had in Dothan as a down payment on the school. The students who were unable to pay money were to work their way, and most of the children lived with families in the community. There was too little money for all the poor children. Times were hard, and they couldn't make the school support itself, so it was lost. Papa and Mama were foreclosed, and their house was boarded up. They lost two horses and a buggy, and most of their possessions. But they did not give up, because they felt they were included in God's plan.

Then Papa got a church in Clio, where I was born in 1909. I was named Sarah Lucille for my mother's mother. I was very little when I was born; they had to hold me on a pillow, I was so tiny. Mama and Papa were still having financial troubles, but Mama was Papa's inspiration. We lived in Clio for a year, and then when I was about two years old, the conference sent Papa to Troy, where we had more lean times. The next year we moved to Andalusia, where Beatrice started to school and my brother James was born in September.

Later that fall, we moved north to Birmingham, where we lived for about five years. In Birmingham, my brother J.D. (Judge David) was born in 1914 and my sister Elizabeth (Lib) was born in 1917. The panic of 1913 and the sinking of the *Titanic* happened while we lived there, and the terrible rains of July 1916, that ruined so much of the cotton crop. Those were the days of King Cotton. The boll weevils ate up so much cotton in those years that many of the tenant farmers moved up north.

The first time as far back as I can remember, is when we lived there, in Birmingham. We lived in the parsonage of Papa's church, about two blocks from Patterson School. Before I was old enough to go to that school, I remember my oldest sister and brother dropping me out of a tree. They had climbed this tree in the backyard, and Beatrice carried me up too. I was a baby at that time. Beatrice wasn't but about six years or so older than me and couldn't hold me. She said, "Oh, she's slipping!"

Albert was on the ground. He said, "Let her come." Now he was about three or four years older than me. Can you imagine him going to catch me falling out of the tree? We were at least six feet up, and to me it seemed like it was high. Of course I hit the ground. It knocked the breath out of me, and they started screaming, and Mama came out and tore them up.

The next thing I got into was our outdoor johny. It had a big hole in it, and I went out to use it, and fell through the hole. Mama to the rescue. They had to pour water all over me outside, and everything. I was always into something. I guess I must have been kind of inquisitive about things and always falling into some kind of mess.

Finally I grew up and got old enough to go to school. As minister's children, we were not allowed to fight. We had to take everything they put on us, because we were supposed to be examples. That was hard for me, because I always felt like self-defense was my priority. We'd come home every day, beat up. They just took advantage of us because they knew we wouldn't fight. All the children would jump on us when they got ready. During that time my brother wore a middy blouse and Buster Brown suit, and I wore a middy blouse dress. They would tear off our collars, but Mama would just sew them back on. I had some pretty shoes that I was so proud of; they were patent leather bottoms and red tops, kind of bootees. My aunt Frankie had bought those shoes for me, and I wore them to school. They threw me down and ripped the red from the black.

Doll Baby did it. Doll Baby and his older sister Frankie lived not too far from us, and their mother was a big member of Papa's church. I can't recall what his real name was, but Doll Baby was his nickname.

Mama did get mad that day. When Mama was mad, she would say, "Diedaddy." That was Mama's curseword. When she said, "Diedaddy," we knew we were going to get tanned or somebody was going to get something. So we came in that day all ragged and muddied up from falling on the red clay road, and Mama said, "Diedaddy" when she saw us. She said, "From now on, I want you to defend yourselves."

When she said that, boy, oh boy, I knew what "defend" meant. That day when school turned out, we caught Doll Baby and Frankie, and Albert threw them down, and I got dirt and put it in Doll Baby's Buster Brown cap. They were well-dressed children; their mama really fixed them up pretty. I put dirt in that cap, and a tin can was there somewhere, and I got some water out of somebody's hydrant, and stirred it up in his cap, and put it on his head. We took his collar off, and he was screaming bloody murder. Frankie ran like a rabbit, screaming like a haint was after her.

That evening, their mother came to our house. She was hot! She told my mama, "I'm surprised at *the preacher's* children, jumping on Doll Baby and tearing up his clothes." Mama said to her, "Sister Ellis, come in. I can show you clothes that I haven't sewed yet, that your children tore off of my children, and I have never gone to you to complain, because children will fight, and then they will be friends."

Mrs. Ellis said, "Well, I want you to whip them, and if you don't, I will."

Mama said, "You will not touch them. Diedaddy, if you put your hands on my child, I'll get you."

Oh, boy, that's all I wanted to hear! I knew then, I was fixed. We had a black doctor named Brawdon, who was very fair and his wife was too. They had two daughters, and they were very fair. During that time, mulattoes were looked up to more than the blacks were. They were the doctor's children, and everybody, all the teachers and everything, catered to them. I hated them. The day after Mama told Mrs. Ellis not to touch us, we got the two little mulatto girls. Now they had never bothered us; they were just cutie pies. But we were going to let them know. We got in behind them and ran them down, but we didn't catch them, because those girls flew. We ran them down and threw rocks at them, so they went back and told the teacher the next day.

This is when the principal called me into his office. I was a little tiny thing, only six years old, and he was tall and jet black. It was in the wintertime, and he had a potbellied stove, great big old round stove that was just roaring. What I couldn't understand was why the teacher couldn't have taken care of a little old thing like me for throwing rocks at those two little old pets, instead of sending me to the principal's office. He said, "I understand you picked a fight, threw rocks at the Brawdon girls." I started crying. He said, "I ought to put you in that heater." And this fire was roaring. You can imagine my fright. But he said, "I'll tell you what, I'm not going to bother you now, but you come back this afternoon." That was in the morning time.

We always walked home from Patterson School to get our lunch. When I got home, I told Mama that I felt bad and didn't want to go back to school. I didn't want to face Mama with the truth. She said if I was sick, she would give me a dose of castor oil. I hated that stuff and told her I didn't feel that bad, so she said, "Well then, you don't feel too bad to go to school." I went on back, and the teacher sent me right back down the hall. When I got back to the principal's office, I don't know why, but I thought of a lie on my daddy. The principal got his strap. I looked up at him and said, "Professor Wilson, my daddy said you're too big to be picking on a little girl like me." You know I didn't get a whipping? He looked at me, and he couldn't do it.

About twenty years later, I saw him at a high school closing, over in Alabama, same Professor Wilson. I introduced myself to him, and he remembered that incident. He was speaking at the graduation exercise, and he brought that up in his speech. He said, "That little girl, that told me that her father said I was too big to be picking on a little girl like her, is in this audience now. From that day on, I have never whipped a little girl."

Did we stop throwing rocks at those little pets after that? No. But they stayed out of our way and put out that we were the worst children in town. That preacher had some terrible children.

Beatrice started working for a white lady named Mrs. M. M. Peterson when she was around twelve. She would work after school, go over there and help clean up and just do whatever Mrs. Peterson told her to do around the house. Mrs. Peterson's mother was an invalid, and Mrs. Peterson worked. Beatrice kind of saw after her mother. She made about a dollar and a quarter a week, and that was very good for us. Mrs. Peterson didn't have much money, but she taught Beatrice as if she were her own child. And Mrs. Peterson would give my sister some of her old clothes, and Mama would fix them so she could wear them.

Beatrice would wear spool shoes given to her by the white ladies. Her feet were as big as the ladies', but because she was just a child, it was hard for her to walk upright on those high heels, and she walked on the sides of her shoes instead. Her feet were cold the whole winter and were frostbitten.

She would walk from Woodlawn to Avondale to school often without food until she got home in the evening. Mrs. Peterson bought her books for a term or so. When there were no books, Beatrice would help some of the other children with their lessons, to be able to study in their books. She had to use wrapping paper and sack paper to write on.

In the meantime, Mama had a job for some people that didn't stay too far from us. They had this big colonial home set back from the street. Mama would carry my brothers James and J.D. with her to work for these people, and they had a little boy around about his age. We got his clothes for Jim and J.D. One day, some of that boy's little white friends teased him about those little nigger boys at his house. So he defended them; he said, "They are not nigger boys. That's Jim and J.D." They played together.

After that, we moved down on the Gate City streetcar line. Papa rented a storefront house, and opened up a store to supplement the small salary he received from the church. We lived in the back.

Mama's baby sister Frankie came to live with us. She was very pretty but she was wild for those times. She liked to dance and liked parties and staying out late. Mama had her to understand, "My husband is a minister here, and we have to keep the family name good."

But Sister came, and she had poloed her hair. You use hot iron combs to press your hair. A black woman had perfected this hair grease and stuff to make your hair straight. And so Sister had straight hair. We just thought she was so pretty. One day she had gone to some wedding or something like that and had some false hair that she'd made a great big ball with. Our little old dog we had got hold to it and carried it off to the coal pile and had chewed on it. She like to had a fit.

But she ran the ice-cream parlor we had on one side of the store. We got pretty chairs, and we have one of those chairs now, over at Lib's, and a table like this. Lib's got the table. We had about four tables and four chairs each. We hand froze the ice cream and sold it; we children cranked the freezer.

In the store part we had weenies that hung from a string. And candy in the showcases. My brother Albert was a little rogue who could reach up there just as smooth, and get a weenie or reach into a case and get him some candy. We wanted to do it, but every time I would reach at that candy, looked like I'd hear Mama walking or somebody coming.

Mama had taught us that the eye of God was everywhere, and I believed her. But I'd always want a piece when Albert got something.

One time Mama had company and she got a big dinner ready. We were out in the backyard where it was shady, and we had made some homemade ice cream for dessert. We had chicken, peas, okra, rice, and cornbread. Papa put the peas and okra and cornbread on my plate, but I didn't want it. I wanted chicken. He said, "You're going to eat that first, and then you get your chicken."

I started hollering. Mama was trying to be nice about it in front of the company, and she said, "Well, just let her wait there until we get to the meat." In those days you didn't eat things all on the plate at once; you had your vegetables first, and then you had your chicken, and then your dessert.

I still hollered, and Papa was going to try to make me eat those vegetables anyway. He got up and went and cut a switch and said, "You are going to eat those peas."

I'm funny about food: if somebody is going to try to *make* me eat, I get so choked up that I can't even swallow. Now I was just a tiny little old brat about six years old, and there was Mama trying to smile and be nice to the company. Papa came with the switch and grabbed me, but Mama jumped up and grabbed that switch and hit him, right in front of the company. Everybody got up from the table but us children.

Mama was so ashamed of herself that she just boohooed. She never did things like that; Mama and Papa never fought. They might argue, but I never even knew that until I got much older, and if they knew we heard them, they would shut up. So I ruined the fine dinner. All the company went home. Sister went in the house and started crying, and Mama went in there and fell across the bed, prostrate. And I ate chicken.

Mama talked about that incident almost until she died. And I still love chicken to this day. But if I had been old enough to understand, I would never have done a thing like that.

Papa had trouble making any profit in the store, because he was so kind and tenderhearted that his customers took advantage of him. I remember one time they came in there and borrowed a kerosene can from Papa, to go over to the next store. A dago had a store on the other corner—Italian—we called them dagos. Went over there buying kerosene from him, and borrowing the can from Papa when Papa sold kerosene himself. Finally the customers owed him so much that he had to close out the business entirely. Folks couldn't pay any money.

That same year the AME Conference assigned Papa to a circuit in south Alabama. We stayed in Birmingham at first. He pastored several churches during that time and could only come home every so often. Money was so scarce that he would send food instead. Beatrice and Albert would go to the express office to pick up the food, and they would sometimes let me tag along. It was exciting to me to see all the boxes of red whiskey and people with sacks, boxes, and suitcases on their way up north. But we were having hard times. We had to gather wood from a hill near our house where they were building a housing project, and coal from the railroad track to cook with.

I remember one Christmas just about that time, when we were so happy. We had a pine tree that Mama had put up. Some children didn't get anything but fruit, but Mama would always figure out some way to get us a toy of some kind. She would get a few little old dolls that were naked and make little clothes to put on them. One of the first dolls I ever had with hair on it, I got that Christmas, but my joy was short-lived. In this house where we stayed, it leaked, actually rained in. It rained that Christmas, all over everything, and because my doll's hair was stuck together with glue, it slid right off. We didn't have anything to stick the hair back on with, and you couldn't pin it on there because it was glass. I had a baldheaded doll after all.

It kept raining in that house, and everything was wet and smelly, and we left there. That was in 1917. By that time, Papa had decided that we should be with him. He had been sent to the Wilsonville church thirteen miles out from Eufala, Alabama, in a place called Batesville, Alabama. He would come home to Birmingham every so often, but there might be two months in between his trips home. He wanted his family with him, so he sent for us.

We were so excited that we were going out in the country where we could holler as loud as we wanted to, and do anything we wanted to; we just imagined the country would be wonderful!

We caught the train. Mama got all the furniture she could together, and had it put on the train. We rode from Birmingham, Alabama, about 180 miles, to Batesville, Alabama. It took us two days on the train. That train was a slowpoke, and then we had to lay over when we got to Montgomery. We stayed there a night and about a half a day in the train station before we left there. Mama had brought quilts, and she spread them out on the floor of the train station, and the children slept on those things. Some of the people said, "Lady, you can't do that," but she did it, because she always looked after her children like a mother hen. In the train station it was just like an exodus of black people traveling, going north to better their lives, because the boll weevil had eaten up all the cotton and ruined their farms. It was pathetic, like you see these people in these countries now, escaping for their lives with the bundles and stuff like that, because they didn't have suitcases. They just had sacks to put their clothes in, headrags on and everything, going north. We ran into all those kinds of people until we caught the train. Cold! That was in January. I can remember that very well, because I was about seven years old. We got hungry as well as cold. Mama told Beatrice to give us something to eat from a basket she had brought. Oh, that food tasted so good!

We rode that train, and when we got to Batesville, one of Papa's members was there to meet us in a two-horse wagon. The wagon had big cracks in the bottom of it. Mama spread those quilts out, and we got in the wagon. We got to this great big farmhouse with a hall that ran clean through it, with half of the house on one side of the hall and half on the other. They had a fireplace almost six feet wide, but you had to sit right there on it because there were great big cracks in the house. You didn't get warm until you got in front of the fire. Oh, the food smelled so good! They were frying smokehouse ham; there was plenty of buttermilk, cornbread, and syrup! Oh, that was the best-tasting food we had ever had! We stayed there with these people until they could get our house ready.

The house they were fixing for us had a hall, too, that went right through it, with no door at either end. At the end of the hall, behind the house, was the kitchen sitting off to itself, with a little boardwalk of two long planks between it and the house. The kitchen was made of logs, but the house was made out of regular lumber. It had been, I understand, in slavery time, an overseer's house on an old plantation, but it had deteriorated. It was called the Big House, and all the other little shotgun houses around it were for the workers, farmers or croppers who worked the fields after slavery time. Some of it had fallen off, but the part that was left was nice and solid. It had a big front yard and two big chinaberry trees, one on each side, and a well. We kept that yard swept. It was stylish in those days not to have grass in your yard. If grass came up in your yard, you chopped it down, and when the leaves fell, you kept it swept. Every Saturday was yard-sweeping time. Across the big front yard and the road, right in front of the house, was the barn and the little outhouse.

On each side of the wide-open hall in the house was a big room. That hall was so wide that if you had closed it in, you would have had another room. As you went in the front door, there were two rooms on the right side, and one room on the other, every room with a fireplace in it. They were two huge bedrooms and a shed room, but all the rooms were used as bedrooms. As you'd go in the front door, the front bedroom was on the left. It was called the company room, and that's where Mama's nicest furniture was. It was like the parlor, but it had a bed in it. My oldest sister Beatrice slept in there, and I just hated her for it. Across the hall, on the right side, was Mama and Papa's room. The little shed room was where the little children stayed, behind Mama and Papa's room. The big boys slept in the kitchen.

That was a good-smelling kitchen, too, sister. We walked from the house across the plank almost thirty-five feet to get to the kitchen. It had a huge fireplace in it. For a cookstove, we had an old range with a broken oven door. The springs were gone on it, so we had to prop the door shut with a stick. There was a big table in the middle, with wooden benches on each side. We ate in there. There were a few shelves, a water shelf to keep the bucket of water and a big pan to wash in. Most of the time we would get our water from the well in the front yard, but sometimes it would run dry, and we'd have to go down the hill and get water from the spring. You could look down to the ground through the cracks in the floor, but it was scrubbed clean.

We had always been very poor in Birmingham. The only thing that brought us to the upper class was my daddy being a minister and my mother being a proud woman and a teacher. She had no inferiority complex at all. She just felt like she was just as good as anybody, and that's the way she taught us to be, independent. We were very proud too; we didn't ever beg. If we would go to people's houses and they were having good food, and we had only had some syrup and bread at home or just some gravy and bread, we said, "No thank you." But we wanted it so bad; it looked so good.

When we moved in our house in Batesville, members of Papa's church came to see us there, and they thought we must have been rich people. Most of them just had a bed, a table built out of lumber, a stove. Some of them didn't even have a stove and would have to cook in the fireplace. Mama had a great big box, built like what you used to put caskets in when people were buried, great big wooden box covered in some kind of flowered material, where she kept our good clothes, and a lock on it. She kept the sugar in there too. Those people just came in and stared at that. We had at that time a lot of clothes compared to those country people. They just had some overall pants that the parents had made by hand, and some of those were very patched up. Mama looked over those children, and she started giving our clothes to them. Now, I didn't like that when I went to Sunday school and saw this girl with my dress on.

There wasn't any school out there, so Mama immediately opened up a school at our house. There were about fifteen children in the school. She used our school books from Birmingham, because we used to have to buy our books in those days. She used our school books and her imagination. Her priority was to teach them how to read and write and figure. Those were the main subjects. Geography and that kind of stuff was secondary. She taught us by giving away our clothes to the neighbors and by the way she ran her school, about sharing what we had with other people, and that still goes a long way with me now.

Mama believed in sharing our food too. When children came to our house, and we'd be having gravy and bread, some of those children who had the good food would enjoy eating the gravy and bread with us. And they didn't say, "No thank you." They sat down there and ate, and argued with us about the gravy and bread. People always loved to come to our house, because Mama made everybody feel at home and made them feel wanted. Of course we children didn't share the same feeling; we didn't like other people coming in and eating our food.

One time a poor white family who were neighbors came by our house, and Mama offered them some breakfast, and the woman said no. But then she said, "Well, I'll take a biscuit and some gravy." Then she sat down there and ate a good breakfast.

We had killed hogs and were fixing some chitlings. This woman sent one of her children down about the time she thought they were done, and asked Mama for some of the chitlings. Mama said, "Those poor folks are probably hungry." So she fixed up some chitlings and some other food and sent it on up. I'm glad of that; I didn't understand it then and would get mad to see Mama feeding other people. But Mama said, "They're human; we'll feed them."

We all grew up to understand that there's somebody always in need, and the more you give, the more you receive. I have a friend right now who says, "Somebody's always giving you something, but nobody ever gives me anything." I say, "That's because you always don't have anything to give anybody." She's just as stingy as she can be. I said, "You've got to give to receive." That's what Mama taught us, but she taught us to do it for its own sake.

My mama believed in sharing within our family and always helping each other. When we were living in Batesville and I was about ten, Mama's sister Frankie, who we called Aunt Sis, wanted to take me up north to live with her. Mama had three sisters, and one of them was named Catherine, and another was Aunt Sis; and she had two brothers named Uncle Bud and Uncle Buddy. Uncle Bud was the oldest one; I think his name was Judge, who my brother J.D.'s named for. The other one was named Roosevelt Lewis. None of the boys had children, but all of the girls had children except Aunt Sis. She adopted a child, and I wanted to go live with her. She would come to see us and she'd have fine clothes. She wanted to take me back to live with her, and I wanted to go.

Mama said no. I just cried. I said to Mama that if I went, there would be more at home for the rest of the children, but she wouldn't have it. And I thought it was cruel of her not to let me go. I didn't know until I was grown and married why she didn't want me to go. Then she told me, said, "If you had gone and lived with Sister, you would have had all the advantages your sisters and brothers didn't have. You might have grown away from them or thought you were better. I wanted all my children to grow up together and have all the same opportunities, the same food, the same love, the same care." I'm glad she did, because I was already kind of a spoiled brat, and I don't know how my mind might have reacted. As a result of our growing up together, we are so close a family that we can sometimes feel when one of us is having trouble or when he's in need. Here comes a letter, with five dollars in it or something.

We all stayed out there in Batesville, and Mama taught, and we had a little farm. Mama didn't know too much about farming, and Papa had three churches way off from each other. He would be traveling with the horse, going from one church to the other. The farming was left up to Mama and the children. In the field we grew some cotton and corn, and then in the garden near the house we grew peas and okra, greens and tomatoes and onions. We had a steer for plowing. We plowed our crops, Lord have mercy! We raised our vegetables and had chickens and butchered our own hogs and carried our corn to the mill to be ground.

We made do. For breakfast we had milk and cornbread, and that was good. We enjoyed that buttermilk! That was before we had our own cow. People would give us milk. We'd get a bucket and go to Miss So-and-So's house whose cow was milking. A lot of people who had two or three cows would have milk left over. If we didn't have that, it was syrup and bread. Sometimes in the real lean days, we would have gravy and bread. Mama would take some lard and brown the meal in it and put in salt and pepper and make gravy. Once it got so bad with us that we went out and picked blackberries and had blackberries and bread, cooked-down blackberries.

When things were going well, for dinner in the middle of the day, we would have boiled peas and maybe some greens, and the same thing for supper. Around hog-killing time we would have some fresh pork, and in the winter while the salt pork and smoked ham and sausage lasted, we would have some of that from time to time. Sometimes we would have chicken. The lean time of year for us was in the late summer or fall, when we had used up the last year's corn for meal, and most of the vegetables were gone from the garden.

We went through so many traumatic times as far as food was concerned. We children weren't as aware of it as Mama was, and Mama had to take care of these problems most of the time, because Papa would be away at one of his churches, or at a conference. One time down in Batesville, I remember, things got hard, and we didn't have any meal. Papa was gone, and Mama was just worried to death. We were always proud people who didn't beg. If people offered things to us, we would go and get them, but we would never ask. Because we were thirteen miles out in the country, there was nobody we could work for. We didn't have anything to carry to town to peddle— chickens or eggs or vegetables—we just couldn't buy anything to eat. We had some corn in the field, but it was only half dry, not dry enough to shuck and carry to the mill, but too hard to boil.

Down in the bottomland by the railroad tracks, we raised our corn. Mama went down in the field, and she was praying, "Lord what can I do?" It was getting dark, but she was down there looking in the field to see if she could find some old dry peas, or some sort of thing. She pulled an ear of corn and looked at it hard, and the idea came to her to take some ears home and grind the corn in our meat grinder. She came up the hill from down in the bottom, carrying the corn and singing that hymn about "Jesus included me. When the Lord said, 'Whosoever will,' He included me too."

We ground and sifted that corn, over and over, until we shook out enough to make a great big hoecake. It was kind of grainy, but sweet! That was some of the sweetest cornbread that I have ever tasted, and we had bread to last until the corn got dry enough to mill. Mama said she just knew the Lord wasn't going to let us starve. With all of that trouble, I cannot remember any time when we hung our heads or went around like we felt sorry for ourselves or went to bed hungry.

That was a beautiful life, tough as it was. In all of our childish fights, there was always Mama to come home to, to help us reason things out. She would tell us why we shouldn't, or what we should have done. It really made a difference. We always had each other to practice on, too. The whole family worked hard together, and we were happy because we had family and love.

Every day at dawn we would get up and do our chores. In the summer, the first thing we would do would be go get hogweed in croker sacks for the hogs. That's all they ate all summer, except for the slops. Wasn't much of that except dishwater, because we ate up all the food. If we had any other animal like a horse or mule, he was fed. Then we would milk the cow. We all had something to be doing; somebody would get water from the well or from the spring way down at the bottom of the hill. The boys would be getting the wood or helping get the hogweeds too. After our chores, we would come in the house and clean our rooms and have breakfast. Then we would tear off to school, running those five miles over hills and creeks, with me carrying our lunch in a bucket—cornbread with syrup over the top.

In Batesville, before we moved away, they had finally got a school, about five miles from our house, so Mama stopped teaching. We would walk those five miles to a school where a teacher who didn't know as much as Mama was a public school teacher. It was in a church. This lady's name was Miss Easter. My brother James was something else. She'd start to teach him to say a word, and he'd say, "I can't say that word. My mother pronounces it this way." She tore his behind up, so that's one time Mama went to school. That woman had said "tow" instead of "to." The teacher didn't bother me, because I knew just about as much as she did. James was under me. So she didn't help us too very much. We got most of our lessons at home with Mama, after we came home from school.

After supper at night, we would get our lessons by a lighter knot. It's a knot that comes off a fat piece of pine, part of a limb, and we would burn that in the fireplace to see. We would lie down on our stomachs in front of the fire, to get our lessons. Mama and Papa never had to push us, except maybe for Albert. We all *wanted* to get our lessons, because we didn't want to be at the foot of the line. Mama was right there with us all the time, and she would sit down and tell us stories and motivate us. We were the richest poorest people you ever saw.

I was always ambitious, always imagining I was going to be a great lady. I would say, "I'm going to be rich and have this, that, and the other. When I get grown, I'm going to marry a rich man and have pretty clothes, and I'm not going to have to work." I wanted a girl and a boy, and that's all the children I wanted, with the boy the oldest.

I did know this—I knew I had to study. I knew about education, and I wanted it. If I had had the opportunity young people have now, I would have had my Ph.D. But in those days you had to work and scuffle and work and scuffle, to get what little bit you did get. But what I got, I was determined to get the best of. I was going to excel in whatever it was that I did, even if it was only cooking cornbread. I learned how to cry, when I thought tears would get what I wanted, and I learned how to be defiant when there were things I thought were wrong. In going to school, when there was a math problem on the board and I copied off somebody else's paper, I wanted to know how to explain how I got that answer, so I couldn't cheat even when I wanted to. I remember when we got into fractions, I stayed up all night long because I couldn't understand them, and the teacher couldn't explain. So I stayed up all night with lighter knots going in the fireplace, figuring out how to work those fractions. Decimal fractions were the same way. Once I got it, I had it.

If it was time for the crops and you weren't at school, you were either chopping cotton, hoeing cotton, replanting corn, or hoeing around the corn. We had to do a lot of hoeing, because we didn't have sharp-enough plows. Those guys that had good plows, and those men that were sure-enough farmers, they could plow and cover the grass in their fields. But our old plows wouldn't do that, so we had to use the hoe to get the grass.

I learned how to plow. I asked my brother Albert to teach me, even though Papa didn't want his girls to plow. Albert and I would switch. We'd be down in the bottom, and Albert would put on my dress and do the hoeing, and I would put on his pants and plow. All anybody standing on the hill would see would be the pants plowing and the dress hoeing. Papa would sometimes stand up there and look down to see what was going on, and he would see those pants going behind the plow. That was me! He finally found out that I knew how to plow, because when Albert would run away, I would do the plowing. The only hard thing about it to me was to hold the plow on a hillside where there were a lot of rocks, to keep it steady. But I did it. We grew cotton, corn, peas.

You know, I used to get on our cow when we had corn, and ride the cow to the mill. I was eleven years old, riding that cow to the mill about five miles up and down the hills with no saddle, and a cow is slick. Mama would put the corn in a long bag, two pecks maybe on one side, and two pecks on the other, and throw it across the shoulder of the cow. I had to hold that up to keep it from sliding down the cow. The old cow's name was Buck because he was butt-headed. I rode Buck one day and the corn slid off. I couldn't get it up on him. So I slid off over his head and got the corn and put it up on him and took him and tied him to a fence and got up on the fence and got on him. I don't know how I untied him, but I sure did it. I think that whatever we have to do, the Lord fixes somehow or another and gives us strength to do what we have to do. I was nothing but a little thing, but I didn't think about crying or running to somebody. I knew I had to get that corn—I was responsible to get that corn to the mill and back home.

When Mama would go off and leave us there and leave chores for us to do, I'd always do what she asked me to do, and something extra. My brother used to jump on me and try to stop me and say I was just doing that to get bragged on. But I just wanted to make my mama proud of me. I always wanted to do more than what I was asked to do. I'm that way now. That has been my philosophy all my life—to do more than I'm asked to do.

We older girls would nurse the babies while Mama worked in the field. Later on, when we moved closer to Eufala, Mama would work in town, and the oldest girl at home would take care of the babies all day. Mama would put the tiny baby on a pallet, and whoever was the nurse wasn't to move him but just feed him cornbread and bacon drippings, mashed up, and give him some syrup and water in a spoon. The one taking care of the baby would go to the spring to get water and wash the diapers and leave them in a tub of clean water for Mama or an older sister to wash when we got home. When Mama or the older sister looked in that water, she better not see anything. Those diapers had to be white as snow. She would finish them up and hang them up to dry.

When we moved from Birmingham, Lib was a baby and I was about seven years old, and I nursed her. I would sit on the steps with the baby in my lap and the baby food all mashed up—gravy and bread or pot liquor or whatever—on a plate. One time I was feeding her, and I had stolen an egg and fried it, and put it in the plate with the baby food. The plate was sitting on the step, and the rooster came up under the steps while I was feeding the baby. I looked down there, and there was that rooster eating a fried egg. I looked in my plate. It was gone! Honey, I was so mad that I dropped the baby in the dirt and got a rock and hit that rooster. Those feathers flew every which way.

My baby sister Catherine was the only one of us born in Batesville, and she was born in about 1919. We called her Baby. When Catherine got bigger, she and Lib were real close. Catherine was outgoing, but Lib was bashful. When I had grown up and moved away from home, I used to make Easter dresses for Catherine and Lib, and I'd always have a blue and a pink, the same size. They would have to make the choices. Lib was always self-effacing, and she would let Catherine choose first. Catherine always chose the pink. She was much fairer than Lib was, and so Lib thought the pink would look better on her.

Now Beatrice was the ideal minister's child, neat and clean and everything, but I was a tomboy. I could climb any tree my brothers would climb; I could ride a horse, mule, cow; plow; all those things. Mama always thought I was never going to do anything in the house, be a housekeeper, because I liked the outside so much. I did learn how to keep house and do all those things, but not when I was very young.

Beatrice would do all the cooking, and she was a great reader. She loved novels. She'd get hung on a story and forget about the dinner. When they would ring the bell at noon and we'd be coming home from the field to get dinner, we'd see a big white smoke jump up out of the chimney. That would be Beatrice; she would have just started the fire to cook.

Mama liked to read novels too, and we all did. She'd get them from the people she worked for. Any book or any piece of paper that had anything to read in it, we read it. We all were readers, even Albert. Mama would sometimes go to sleep with a storybook, when she had read us part of it, and we wanted to know what the other part was, we'd slip it out of her hands so she'd wake up. She'd say, "Put that book back."

We wore our clothes all week and washed them on Friday night. To get the clothes clean, you used lye, and you boiled them. I just had one dress, and I wore it freshly ironed and starched on Sunday, and then all through the week. Of course when I got home from school and on Saturdays, I put on some old kind of working clothes and saved my dress. On Saturday we swept the yard and cleaned the house, then had our baths Saturday night. I can't remember having a bath between Saturday nights, although we always washed our feet before we went to bed in the summertime, because we went barefooted. Everybody washed in the same water, because you had to go down under the hill to the spring to get water. Papa would let us wash his feet, and I loved that. He had the prettiest feet, I thought. He was real dark, but his feet were brown and fat. He always wore boots, though, high-top shoes; I don't ever remember him wearing oxford-type shoes. We would always pull off those boots and wash his feet for him.

Every Sunday morning when we would get up, we would have family prayer, and that was the thing that I detested. Papa would sing a hymn and pray the longest prayer telling God everything. We would be smelling the breakfast on the table, and we would want to eat so bad. I said I wasn't ever going to have prayer on Sunday morning when I grew up.

After breakfast, Papa would call us in and shine our shoes. He had a last that he had made, and we'd put our little feet up on it for him to shine. He was so rough that you could hardly hold your foot on there. There was a concoction that he had made up, soot and syrup and lard, that he used as polish. Can you imagine what our shoes looked like when we walked out into the dust? Everything would stick to them.

When we had put on our clothes, we would walk out to be examined, and Mama would name us. My oldest sister she would call Cleopatra, and she would model, and then I was the queen of Sheba and would model. I always hated that hair-combing business because I had thick, long, kinky hair and would scream when they combed it. My sister Beatrice was the roughest hair-comber I ever saw.

Albert was Prince Albert, of course, and his pants were made out of the bottom of Papa's pants. Because Papa was a minister, his clothes had to look nice. Papa weighed 310, and Mama would put a V in his pants to make them bigger as he grew stouter, but he would wear out the V. When he wore the seat out of his pants and Mama couldn't do any more patching and the coat couldn't hide it all, she would make pants for the boys out of the bottoms. The material was serge, so it would make nice pants for the boys.

When we were all dressed and Mama had named us all, we would go to Sunday school and stay there all day. Albert was always getting into something, so what my Daddy would do sometimes when Albert was being naughty is take him up in the pulpit with him. Then when the service was over, Papa tore him up. We couldn't talk, we couldn't go to the bathroom, we had to stay in church until it was over, no matter how long they sang or how long Papa preached.

I always liked to be in church, because that's where I would see my friends and we would get a chance to talk and play when church was out. Sometimes the old people carried food there, and we stayed all day. But we would have a break to eat.

Mama would take us through the woods sometimes on Sunday afternoons and show us the handiwork of God—the dogwood trees and honeysuckle, the colors in all the flowers. She could grow anything; she had a green thumb. She was artistic, and she could work rings around any of us. She could always make people feel like they were more than they were, make you feel good about yourself.

My oldest brother, who was really a mischievous boy, couldn't stay still anywhere. He'd run away from home, and then come back and tell some of the wildest stories of his experiences. I wanted to follow him so bad! I wanted to see the world, and he promised to take me. When I got large enough to travel with him, he said, "You're a girl, and I come in contact with all kinds of people saying all kinds of ugly, nasty things. I don't want my sister to be exposed to that." So I lost out on running away from home. I would always know when he was going because he would sing a song, "This time tomorrow I won't be here, and the world can't do me no harm." That meant he was leaving.

During that time the old folks said that children shouldn't eat eggs because it made you womanish. But we'd steal them. The hens would lay all in the woods, and we would find the nests. We had a way of cooking them. Albert thought of this; he knew everything about how to steal and get by with things. We would get a rag and wet it and wrap the eggs in it and dig a hole and build a fire on top of it. That wet rag would steam the eggs done. Sometimes, if we felt like it, we would tell Mama that we found a hen nest with two eggs in it, when there might have been a dozen or more. One time Albert—we had an iron kettle, always sitting by the fire and boiling—Albert stole some eggs and put them in the kettle. My brother James and I saw him when he did it. The eggs got done, and somehow Mama disappeared, and we got them out and ate them. Albert came looking for his eggs and couldn't find them. He jumped on us, but he couldn't tell Mama why. We'd always do something like that, take advantage of one another.

My brother Jim was sweet and very dignified and sophisticated, from a little boy. He was bowlegged and brown and always had a bumpy face. Jim always looked just like a professor, and I'd always be playing tricks on him. We always played conjure, and I always conjured Jim. I would dig a hole in the ground and put anything in it, a

top or a piece of glass I'd find, or a button or two, and then I'd ask him
to jump over it. He'd jump over it, and I'd say, "I've got you." Then he
would just cry, and I'd get things out of him, special things like his
dessert.

Out there in Batesville, there were some children called Lawson.
About four of those children came to Mama's school. The eldest was
around sixteen or seventeen years old, trying to learn how to read and
write. It was kind of pitiful, but they did; Mama taught them how.
Some of them would use snuff in their lip. They'd go down into the
woods where the bathroom was, for recess, and they'd dip snuff. I
always wanted to be a big girl and do like the big girls were doing. I
went down there behind them and begged them for a dip of snuff.
They gave it to me. I have never gotten so drunk! Nasty drunk! I
might have swallowed it, I don't know, but I couldn't even spit. I just
had to open my mouth and let it run out. They left me down in the
woods and went back to the house. Mama asked them where I was, but
they all said they didn't know. Finally one of my brothers found me and
said, "This poor child is so sick." They didn't know what to think. She
made some tea. I was just snuff drunk. From then on, I never wanted to
see a dip of snuff.

We always wanted to go play, and it was a treat to go visit some other
child and play. It was good to have sisters and brothers, because when
you couldn't go somewhere and visit, you could play with them. We
played house. In the woods or in the yard, we would use broken pieces
of glass and china for plates. Some of them had pretty flowers on them,
and those were our dishes. We would pull grass up, that had a lot of
root to it, and plat the roots for hair, to make dolls out of them. We
would be the mamas, and they would be our children. We would put
them to bed, and our husbands would come from work—the boys, you
know—and we would fix food for them—mud pies. We used a lot of
imagination.

CHAPTER TWO

Life in the Batesville Neighborhood
(1917–1920)

W
e had good neighbors in Batesville, a good community life.
It was a rural area eighteen miles from Eufala and five miles
from the nearest store. It was beautiful farming land with
rolling hills and flatlands. It was quiet out there. You would hear people calling each other, calling hogs, calling cows. In the fall you'd hear
gunshots, when the men were out hunting possums and squirrel. At
night we'd hear the dogs barking and cows lowing and screech owls.
We were afraid of screech owls and would tie a knot in our sheet to stop
them from screeching.

Where we lived, there were about six families living within the ra-
dius of a mile. The church was a kind of center; it was the meeting
place for the community. Neighbors would come by our house and sit
and visit and trade gossip. There were no radios or newspapers, so
when anybody had a magazine or newspaper, they'd gather around to
talk about the news.

During the fall we'd go out in the woods and find hickory nuts and
black walnuts. In summer we'd find wild grapes—muscadines—and
blackberries. Mama would make wine and jelly. People had chinaberry
trees in their front yards for shade, and when the berries got ripe, the
birds would eat them and get drunk. We children would catch them
and wring their necks and then roast them and eat them.

Most of the families out there had a father and a mother, but some of
the women had children by men they weren't married to. The wife
accepted it, because this woman and her children did the farm work, so
the wife got to stay in her house and do housework. They both lived on
the same plantation. One of our neighbors, Mr. Crews, had his wife

and his concubine and his outside children. They did the farm work, and his wife stayed home. He couldn't read or write a scratch, but he was a good farmer and had the cane mill where we all made our syrup. Mr. Crews also did a lot of hunting, and he would have traps out for coons and possums and things like that. He would get them and the mailman would pick up the hides. So Mr. Crews would raise some money on that.

Mr. Crews had his cane mill and kept syrup all year. We'd take our cane there for grinding in the fall, and then they would boil it and dip the skim off, and that skim is what they made the moonshine out of. Sometimes hogs would get in it and get drunk as Cooter Brown. And with his syrup, if you made fifty gallons of syrup in his mill, he got a fourth of it. He knew how to measure that out.

He always kept two or three barrels of good sugarcane syrup that smelled so good in there. I can just smell it now. He would tilt the barrel up and pour it in the gallon jugs made of pottery. You would use a corncob stopper. I used to pull out the stopper and suck it, and then stick it back in.

When we first moved out to Batesville, he was fixing some lye hominy. I had never heard of it until we moved out there and they sent a bucket of it to Mama, saying if we liked it, we could get some more. We liked it, and so Mama told me to go back and tell them we did and that if they had some more, we would appreciate it. Since I'd never heard of it before, I repeated it all the way, so I could remember what I was going for. "Lye hominy, lyominy, lahominy, lamimy, laminy." By the time I got there, I was saying, "Fahmily." They couldn't understand me, but I had the bucket and said, "Send us some more of that formily cause we liked it."

They said, "Formily?"

I said, "That white stuff that you sent over in the bucket."

She said, "Oh, you're talking about hominy."

I said, "Oh, yes ma'am." So we got some hominy.

The way they made it was that they took dried corn and put it in one of these old black iron pots, what they called washpots, and put Red Devil lye in the pot with the corn and boiled it until the husks loosened up. Then they took it out and washed the husks off and put it back in the pot and boiled it again, just in clean water. That was getting the lye part off. That corn would turn white, and it was delicious, especially if you fix it with bacon drippings. Use an old tin can as a kind of chopping thing, cook it in bacon drippings and chop it a little bit and add pepper to it, and it is delicious. I could even eat it cold.

During the summertime, our hogs kept plump on hogweed. Then when the corn came in and we were going to get ready to kill, we put them in a stall with a floor to it, high up with holes in it. The mess could drain out through those holes. We would give them corn in that stall for so many days until the fat got hard and pretty and clean. We kept corn in their straw, and they ate as much as they could for about three weeks. By that time, they would be fat enough to kill.

Everybody would kill hogs around the same time, because you had to wait for the real cold weather to come in the fall so you could cure your meat without having it spoil while you were curing it. Nobody had cold storage back then. Big farmers would kill a number of hogs, but since Papa was just a half-hand farmer, since he was off preaching most of the time and Mama and we children would have to do most of the farming, we didn't kill but about two or three hogs in a year. The neighbors were all so kind. All the neighbors would send someone from their family over to whoever was butchering that day, to help, and they'd all get a piece of fresh meat. You'd share it out. We would broil liver over the coals; that tasted so good! We would all work together, every one of us down to the little toddlers who had to go bring in one stick for the fire or something. I always thought the girls had the worst time, because we had to do most of the work.

We would clean the chitlings and cook them and the lights or hashlets all in a pot together with onions. You cut it all up in there and it automatically made brown gravy. With a little thickening in it, you put it on biscuits or over top of rice and it tasted *good*, just delicious. We would eat the brains too, scrambled up with eggs.

After the hog had been killed, they would pick the hair off him and take his head and open that up and get the brains out. You would put them in a dish and pour scalding water over it, and then pull all the little membranes off. Then the hog ears and head were cleaned—you cleaned the wax part out of the ears, and you opened up the nostrils and cleaned and scrubbed them. You put the head and feet in a pot and cooked them until the meat fell off the bones, then pick the bones out and work all the meat up together and ground it up in a meat grinder with peppers and spices to make head cheese.

From the backbone and other lean parts, some of the parts they didn't cure, we would make sausage. You would cut that out and grind it up with some fat and seasonings. Then we would turn the little intestines inside out and scrape them and wash them clean, then stuff them with the sausage. Sometimes you would smoke the sausages, and sometimes put them in lard. To make your lard, you would cut the fat off the hog and put that in a pot over the fire until it melted down and made cracklings. Then we put the sausages in our lard cans and poured that boiling lard over the sausages. The hot lard would cook those things and they would stay preserved in there until you used up enough lard to get down to them. That was the best way to keep the sausage, because if they were smoked, the children could go in the smokehouse and take some, but nobody wanted to reach down into the lard can to get any. The housewives would know just how much sausage was down there and could go down into the can and get it.

They'd kill it and pack it down in salt. It stayed in that salt for so many weeks. Then they would take it out of the salt, wash it off, and put it in the smokehouse and let it dry with oak chips making a steady smoke.

We would eat *fine* on the fresh pork for a couple of weeks while they were curing the hams and shoulders and sides and all that. It would depend on how cold the weather was, how long you could keep the fresh meat. The salted and smoked meat would last from then until round about April or May. We never did have meat all during the year, though some other people did the year round. That was some good meat; you could *smell* it cooking. Now you can hardly taste the stuff you buy, no more than smell it.

One time we had a pig we called Squatty Rod, that was the smallest pig of the litter. When they were born, we had thought that he was going to die. We called him Squatty Rod because his bowels moved often, real soft, like squirt, squirt, squirt. He had a long nose and whiskers that made him look lean and skinny, while all his sisters and brothers were fat. But we loved old Squatty Rod and would always give him extra corn. He grew into a fine fat hog. Then when he was two years old, Papa decided to butcher him. You talk about somebody crying, swearing that they would never eat a piece of his meat—as much as we loved meat! It turned our stomachs to think of eating his meat because we loved him, and also because we could just see him back when he got his name.

We killed three hogs that year, and what Mama did was tell us every time we ate a piece of pork, that this wasn't Squatty Rod we were eating. I know that we had to have eaten him sometime, but we never knew when. When they salted the meat down and hung it up to dry, we couldn't tell Squatty Rod from anybody else.

One time we had a field full of peas, crowder peas. We had that to eat on during the winter, and seed peas to use the next year. Mama sent us down to the field to pick the dry peas, and Sister Crews came along. There were a lot of "Sisters" back then. She was one of Mr. Crews's daughters and was hunting her milk cow. She wanted us to go with her, and then she would come back and help us pick the peas we were supposed to take home. Instead of staying in the field as we were supposed to, we decided to go with her and help. It was dark when we came back with the cow. There in the field the sacks were lying in the rows. So we picked them up and came on home for supper. As we came walking up, we could smell that supper. Mama asked us where we had been, and we told her we'd helped Sister hunt her cow. Mama said, "All right, but you go back in the back room, because we've got some business to tend to before you eat your dinner." Lord, I felt like Judgment Day was coming. Mama would whip you so sweetly, but she'd get a switch and looked like she would cut your hide off. She'd say something nice, and . . . POW!! Talking about how she loved us. I knew she was going to hit me on my buttocks, and I decided to do something about it. We had a little closet we put our dirty clothes in, and I went in there and got one of Mama's long skirts and put it on, and got one of the pillows from the bed and put it under there. There wasn't any light in the room but from the lighter knot in the fireplace. The one lamp we had was in the kitchen, so it was kind of dim in this room, like candlelight. She came in from the kitchen, and I asked to be whipped first. So she started up and hit that pillow. Boop! Boop, boop! Well, I got so tickled I couldn't help but start laughing, just screaming laughing. She couldn't understand it—she was just tearing that pillow up. She said, "Beatrice, bring that lamp in here!" She knew something was wrong, but when she saw me with that pillow on, she dropped that switch and started screaming. She was so tickled that she couldn't whip me any more. Every time she looked at me, she'd bust out in a big laugh, and Albert escaped a whipping too. I had to think of something, because I didn't want that whipping, and I was *hungry*. And old Sister Crews was sitting there laughing, and I told Albert that we better get her.

Sister Crews's father had a son named Cliff. Cliff Crews was Beatrice's boyfriend, but I loved him for my own boyfriend. So he called me his little girlfriend. I thought that was something. They had a big meeting going on down at the church, a camp meeting that they had every year. Every night Beatrice would come back with a big stick of peppermint candy that Cliff had bought her. I got jealous, so when he came to get Beatrice to go to church, I caught him and said, "You are always getting Beatrice candy and don't ever buy me anything."

He said, "Well, I'm going to get you something." He slipped off from church that night and came back to the house. I was there tending babies. Cliff came back with a stick of candy and said, "Now don't you tell Beatrice, because I don't have but that one stick."

I kept that candy, and when Beatrice came back home, I showed her my stick of candy and told her Cliff brought it to me. She just thought he lied; she wasn't thinking about how I might really like him, because I was just a little old girl. Then he wanted to know why I told Beatrice. I said, "Well, she always told me how you gave her some candy, and I'm your girl too." He kind of laughed, but he didn't get me any more candy.

One night . . . we had a shutter window in our house. There was no glass in it; you opened it out. In the front room was the shutter window. Cliff was there visiting Beatrice. Beatrice wanted me out of the room, but Mama said, "What have y'all got to talk about that Sarah can't hear?" I stayed in the room and listened. I kept the fire going so I could see what was happening. Somehow or another, I went to sleep. He had to be gone from there by nine o'clock, so it must have been earlier than that. We had nothing to do out there but go on to bed after we got through with our supper, unless Mama told us a story or something like that. No radio or Victrola or anything. So I went to sleep.

That shutter window was used for my brothers to tee-tee out of, and when the rain would come up and the sun would shine on it, you could smell that odor. Mama had been fussing at them about using that window. Now I had been using it too, but she didn't know about that. While Cliff and Beatrice were courting, I woke up, not realizing that they were there. I got in the window and started my watering, and Beatrice screamed. I like to fell out of the window. That fixed it for me and Cliff; I was no more his little girl. And Beatrice soon got rid of Cliff.

The Corbetts were our other close neighbors. Lena Corbett was my best friend, and they lived right down the road from us. She had a brother named Jesse and one named Jake. Her father was a big farmer out there, Mr. Jim Corbett, very strict on his children. But he was a good farmer and a good provider.

One time Mama and Papa went off to a conference and left us home. In the meantime, Beatrice was living in Eufala and going to school, and there was Albert—he was home at that time; he hadn't run away again. He decided that we were going to have a chicken dinner. It was around June. Mama had left the food for us to cook, but no chicken. We had lots of chickens, and the hawks would catch some of them. Lena Corbett, my good friend, decided she and her brothers and sisters wanted to get in on the chicken dinner too, because their daddy had gone to the same place as my mama and daddy, and they had a lot of chickens. Albert said, "Now we don't have much lard to fry those chickens with, so we'll boil them." So we killed the chickens, about five or six of them, and cleaned them and put them in the washpot. My friend Lena wanted the heads, to cook, and so we gave them to her—a bad mistake.

Albert decided that we needed some dessert. Miss Emma Wilson and her sister lived across the little creek, and they had a watermelon patch with some of the prettiest watermelons you've ever seen. We were some of the only children out there who wore tennis shoes. It was summertime, and most of the other children just went barefooted. Compared to them, we were lucky to have some shoes; we had tennis shoes to wear to church. Now, I don't know why Albert had on his tennis shoes that day, but he did, and he went over to get our dessert. Miss Emma and her sister always marked their watermelons; when they came on the bushes they'd put a cross on them or something, to know from the time they started when they would be ripe. For some reason, Albert lost one of his tennis shoes in the watermelon patch, but he brought us a watermelon. We had chicken going to bed!! We buried the bones and the feathers and everything.

About two days later, Mr. Corbett came to our house and told Mama that we had stolen some of his chickens. Mama said, "No, why would they do that?"

He said, "We found the heads." Lena hadn't gotten a chance to cook the heads, and they had started smelling. She had told on us. In the meantime, Miss Emma came with the shoe.

Papa called Albert and asked him where his tennis shoes were, and he said, "In the house."

So Papa said, "Go get them." Albert couldn't find but one. Papa said, "Is this your shoe?" and Albert said, "Yes sir." So then Papa said, "Well, what was it doing in Miss Emma's watermelon patch?"

"I don't know," said Albert.

And Papa said, "Well, that's where it was, and Miss Emma's biggest watermelon was gone." Papa tore him up, and we got punished about the chicken heads. But Mama and them never noticed any chickens gone from our house; after that, every time Mama and Papa left on a trip, we had us some chickens.

Mr. Corbett was a good provider but a mean daddy. One night we heard Lena screaming, and Mama said, "Good gosh, somebody must be dead or something!" So she ran down to the Corbetts' house. He had Lena stripped, and she was about thirteen then, stripped naked, and her hands tied up to the joists of the house. There wasn't any ceiling up there, just joists, and he was whipping her. Mama said, "If you don't stop, I'll kill you! Shame on you for having that child like that!" Mrs. Corbett was just standing back there grinning. She was the stepmother. He stopped.

Lena decided to run away from home, and I was going with her. We were going to run away to a city and get rich. We got ready and got our little things together, and she came by my house. There was a place in the field, going down toward the railroad, a hill or a ridge. At the bottom of the hill there was a spring of the coolest water you ever tasted, just so nice! And the story went that there was a woman working in the field who got hot and thirsty. She went down to the spring to get a drink of water, and died, so they call the ridge Woman's Ridge. We got as far as that Woman's Ridge and decided we would eat watermelon for our food until we could get to a city. It was getting kind of dark, and we heard a screech owl make that weird sound, "Screereech!" It frightened me so, that I said, "I believe I'm going back home." I was just going to help her run away, but I lost my courage. She started crying and said they were going to kill her if she went back home. I said, "No, they won't. You come on back home with me, and we'll tell Mama. She will stand up for you."

When we got back home, I told Mama what we had done and that I was just going with Lena to keep her company. She said, "Well, that was mighty sweet of you, but it was wrong of both of you. Lena, you just stay here tonight, and I'll go down to your father's house and let him know that you're up here and ask him if it's all right for you to spend the night." So that's how it was.

Lena had an older brother who was crazy about me, named Jesse, and I couldn't stand him. He would try to get up close to me, and I would fight him off. I'd grab up a stick or something to hit him, and he'd just grab the stick. One time I told him, "I want you to stay away from our house. Mama doesn't want anybody around here when she's not here." He said, "We're renting from the same man, so I have just as much right here as y'all do." Way on down the line, Jesse still loved me, until even now. I saw him about ten years ago, and he said, "Sarah, I still love you." I even got engaged to marry him. But that's in the next installment.

There weren't any newspapers around there, but sometimes somebody would get hold of one, and Mama and Papa would read it. Mr. Corbett was well educated and liked to discuss current events. So he would come around to the house sometimes and sit around and talk with Mama and Papa about things. Sometimes they would let us sit in there and listen. I liked to hear those things, because I remembered them too.

The mailman, Mr. Robertson, was the secretary for a lot of the black folks out there who couldn't read or write. He'd ride around there in his buggy and would write their letters for them, fill out their order forms for Sears and Roebuck and Bellas Hess and all those mail-order companies. He knew everybody, and everybody knew him. He could go to sleep, and his horse would know where to stop at the mailboxes.

Mama would peddle eggs and peas. We would sell those good old shelled peas for fifteen cents a gallon and were glad to sell them for that. We'd pick blackberries to sell. Mama started peddling before we moved from Batesville. I guess that's why we couldn't eat any eggs, because she'd get up the eggs and the chickens, fryers, and carry them. She'd sell that to buy sugar, rice, stuff for our hair, coffee, whatever we didn't have on the farm.

One time she went to buy Beatrice some boots that were very stylish at that time, bootees they called them, high tops that were strung up. Beatrice was going to school in Eufala by that time. Mama went to this store and fainted in there because she hadn't eaten anything. All the money she had was about a quarter. besides what it took to get Beatrice some shoes, and she was supposed to get some groceries out of it, too. But she was determined that Beatrice was going to have those shoes. I think between thinking about it and being hungry, she just passed out. Mr. Foy was the owner of that store. It just killed her, but she got those shoes.

I can just see those shoes now, brown, sharp-toes, strung up to here.

Beatrice was tall and skinny, but the boots always make you look like you have big legs. She would wear thick stockings to make her legs look bigger. Beatrice always kept her clothes just as neat, everything in place. I would always wish I had what she had. Mama said you'll get big, but right now Beatrice is the oldest, and she just needs to have more things. I was always climbing trees and slitting on barbed wire, and one time I slid on a sliding board and stuck a pitch fork up in my head. It's a wonder I didn't go crazy. There's a knot up there now. I was always into something.

When times were hard, Mama cried because things weren't going well and she didn't have the things that she wanted for us and for the house, but she always took whatever she had and made the best of it. Even a bone, after all the meat was cut off of it, she could take and boil, go out in the garden and scrape up a few little peas that were left after the harvest, and maybe a last tomato. She would put all those little pieces together and make a soup. It was the best-tasting soup! Sometimes we would be ashamed when people came to eat with us, because we didn't have anything for company food. But Mama would go in that kitchen and find something, and make the nicest meal.

I remember one night when one of our neighbors came over and just stayed to eat. She waited. Mama had a chicken cooking and was trying to cook around until this neighbor left, but the woman said, "I smell something good. I believe I'm going to spend the night." So Mama gave up and called us in to dinner. That woman ate plenty of chicken, and then said, "Lord, I forgot I done left them children home by themselves. I'd better get on back." So she got up and left.

Mama would make syrup-bread cookies sometimes on winter nights. Oh, boy, those were good on cold or rainy winter nights! She would take syrup, if she had some, and she would make some sweet squares out of cornbread. On days when it would be raining and we couldn't go out, she'd make syrup candy or roast some peanuts or some potatoes in the fireplace, cover them up in the ashes. For dinner she would cook a chicken down and have some gravy, and those cookies.

Mama always made cakes for weddings and parties the white people she worked for were giving. At Christmas, she made cakes for those people and for us. When she was making those cakes, she would leave a little dab of batter and let us lick the pans. We would take turns, calling out, "I catch the pan this time." And then somebody else would say, "I catch it next year." And another would say, "I catch it year after next." I vowed that when I grew up, I was going to make a cake and eat the whole thing, and nobody would be able to stop me because I would be grown. I did, too. When I was married to James Hayes, I made a cake and cut it in half and said, "This half is yours, and this one's mine," and we ate it up.

Then the old folks would have little parties sometimes, just to roast peanuts and sweet potatoes in the ashes and make candy. We would sit up there, with Mama and the other old folks in one room talking and the children in another room roasting peanuts and listening to haint stories. Then when we got ready to go home, we would catch the tail of Mama's dress, because if a stick cracked, we would think that was a ghost coming.

Sometimes the women would give a quilting, and we children would go with Mama. They would sit up and have the quilt spread out on the quilting rack, with two or three women on one side and two or three on the other. They would whip a quilt out in a night, and they wouldn't stay late because they were tired. The lady whose quilt it was would have syrup bread. You roll it out like you do biscuits and cut it out in squares and bake it. A lot of the old folks would put it in a flour sack and hang it up on the rafter of the house to keep the children from getting it. If they didn't have any flour, which they didn't have a lot of times, they made it with meal.

In those early days, we used to go out and pick blackberries and make wine for the church, for communion. At Christmastime, Mama would serve wine and cake. We liked the wine, so we'd steal it, but we did it wrong. Instead of getting just a little bit out of the jug and leaving the rest like it was, we poured water in to make it come up to the level. Of course, when Mama got ready to serve some wine out of the bottle we went into, it was vinegar. All of us would swear that we didn't do it, that the Lord would knock us paralyzed, and we just hoped he wouldn't.

During Christmas season, Mama and Papa would go to town and get some apples and oranges for us. Then on Christmas Day, we would each have a shoe box with an apple, an orange, some raisins, and if Mama had enough money, some nuts, inside. And she'd always make each of us a little something, like a rag doll.

One year they got the apples and oranges a week early and locked them up in the box where Mama kept the sugar and our clothes. We could smell those apples, but we still believed in Santa Claus. Albert knew everything, though, and he told us there wasn't any Santa Claus. He said, "Smell those apples in Mama's box. Mama and Papa are going to use those to pretend like they're Santa Claus." We still didn't believe him, so somehow or other he got the key and got into the box. I joined him in eating up the apples.

Mama decided to check on the Christmas things, and then she discovered that all the apples were gone. She and Papa must have gone back to town and gotten some more, because when Christmas Day came, we all got our apples.

Mama kept the sugar in the box or chest where she kept our clothes. I had an act of stealing sugar from there. One day I went in the room and went in the box when she had forgotten to lock it, and got my mouth so full of sugar that I couldn't open it to talk. Mama called me, but I couldn't answer or all the sugar would have spilled out on the floor. I was trying to chew fast to get it down, when she walked in and caught me. When she got through with me, I never stole another grain of sugar. She got a switch and wore me out, saying softly all the while, "Now Sarah, you know better than that. Why did you go in that box and get the sugar, when you knew you weren't supposed to do it? How many times . . . ?" Pow! Pow!

I hated those kind of whippings, with all the talk. I had rather get through with it. My father would get a strap and give us three licks, maybe two, talking along. Whap! And then talk some more, and you didn't know when the next lick would come. Whap! "I want you to be a good girl." Whap! "Why did you do that?" Whap! A lot of times we got whippings for something we didn't do. Somebody would have done whatever it was, but Mama and Papa didn't know who, so Papa would whip us all.

Beatrice would try to whip me sometimes, because we children always had to mind the oldest one, the one our parents left in charge. I never did let Beatrice whip me; I would fight back. One day she got me. We had an iron bed, and she tried to make me do something, and I wouldn't do it. She caught me and had my back going back over this bed. I screamed bloody murder, and just then Mama walked in. I was going to get that sister for that.

I told my brother Albert that I wanted to fix Beatrice. In the meantime, she had laid across her bed to take a nap. She would always sleep with her mouth open, so I got the Vaseline and put a hunk of it in her mouth while it was open, and then called her. She woke up and started screaming with all this sticky stuff in her mouth.

But that wasn't the end of it. Albert came up and said, "Now we're going to do something. She is always wanting to know the answer to things, and we're going to put a chip on each one of her shoulders." I said, "Albert, how are you going to do that?"

He said, "Come on, I'll show you." We went out in this hard front yard, of dry clay almost like pavement. Beatrice was round about fifteen or sixteen years old. Albert said, "I could call your name, and you can't answer."

Well, Beatrice said, "There is nothing you can do to call my name and I can't answer."

He said, "Oh, yes I can. I will put a chip on each one of your shoulders, and one on each one of your feet, and call your name, and you won't be able to answer."

So Beatrice said, "I'll try it." So he put the chips on her shoulders and then on her feet and called her name and snatched her feet out from under her. She fell on that hard pavement, and of course she couldn't answer. That scared me and almost knocked her out.

He got a whipping for that. Mama said, "You could have ruined her." That was the last spanking Beatrice tried to give to me. Because I would run.

Finally I got to be the big boss, and I remember I would try to whip J.D. It took all my might and main to make him go milk the cow. I was so tired when I got through with that boy, he almost got me. That was my last time trying to manhandle anybody. He was so strong! Uh, uh, I left that off. But afterwards, I didn't have any problem with him at all, because I had beat him down that day. I wasn't going to jump on him again, but he didn't know that.

By that time Beatrice was going to school in town. Pretty soon she finished. She was pretty smart; she took the state teachers' examination and passed, and got a school. She went to Geneva to teach down there. The funny thing about it was that she had such a beautiful handwriting, they just assumed that she was white. So they gave her a white school. When she got there they saw she was as black as me; they had to make some quick arrangements to put her in a black school. She was glad to get it. That's where she met Harvey, her husband.

One of Mr. Crews's concubines was named Miss Fanny Ransom, and she would have frolics at her house every Saturday night. She was a tall, slim, real black woman who lived in a little house by herself and didn't have any children, but the other concubine did. Miss Fanny just worked in the field. She had a real neat waist and always wore a skirt and a blouse.

A frolic was like a dance, and of course we couldn't go to it, but it would look like people were having such a good time. Somebody would be there picking a guitar, and they'd all be dancing around and they would be selling sandwiches. Every time a man danced with a person, he would have to treat that girl by buying some of whatever they had, whether it was rabbit or possum or fish or chicken or sweet potato pie or a can of sardines. The more popular a girl was, the more stuff she got, and the mamas would be sitting around the room and be the collector of it. She'd have a pile of stuff to carry home with her.

Miss Fanny borrowed our lamp. Papa came home and wanted to study his Bible. Mama said, "I let Sister Fanny have our lamp." So Papa sent my brother Albert down there to get it, but Albert got down there and got fascinated with the dancing. Then Papa sent me to get Albert, but I got fascinated too. I wanted to get out on that floor and dance like Miss Fanny. The men would spin her around and pop up her dress high.

Papa finally came himself, and Albert and I tore out for home. Papa said, "If I ever catch you hanging around those places again, I'm going to do so and so and so." My mother liked dancing, and when Papa was gone somewhere, she'd prance around and we'd prance around with her.

Dancing at the frolics was kind of like what you call square dancing; you get around in a circle and swing around to different partners while somebody is singing. Songs like, "I got a gal in Kalamazoo." Flap, flap, flap, flap, flappidy flap, they'd be jumping around, and the guys would be swinging them around.

One guy was named Edgar Skipper who was the bully and would always have his forty-five pistol. When Edgar Skipper walked into a party, everybody minded their manners. He would just haul off and shoot up in the top of the house. Pow! And the people would start running and jumping out of the windows. There wasn't any law out there; the closest law we had was in Clayton, Alabama, about fifteen miles away. The sheriff wasn't going to come out there with his two-horse truck or car to a Saturday night frolic. Edgar Skipper came into Miss Fanny Ransom's one night and shot, and the people ran off and left all the food. Some of the boys, including my brother Albert, went in there and got a stomach full of the food for nothing. Finally somebody killed Edgar Skipper.

One of the saddest things that happened out there was to a pretty girl whose parents moved to Montgomery or Birmingham. Her name was Sister Virgin, and the boys were just crazy about her. She had two boyfriends, jealous of each other. She went riding with one, and the other one came up and killed her. That scared me for a long time about having two boyfriends. It's better to have just one, and if he's no good, get rid of him and get another one. Don't mess around with two of them.

The Crawford girls stayed not too far from us, and their father was a big farmer who had a pretty brown wife, part Indian and with long black hair. He was kind of fair, and they had the prettiest children you ever saw. Some of them went to town school during the time Beatrice went, and they really wanted that education, to make something of themselves.

Beatrice said that I was spoiled when I was little. Well, I didn't know I was spoiled, but everybody called me cute, and I was smart in my books and could say these long recitations. Papa liked to carry me with him to his churches. He'd say, "Come on and I'll carry you to church with me," and I'd get in the buggy with him and go. He'd always have me stand up there in church with him, and he'd say, "This is my daughter Sarah." He'd have me read or recite, and everybody was fascinated because they couldn't learn anything like that. They would say, "How could she learn that?" with me so young and could read.

The recitation I still remember was one that Mama taught me. She had learned it as a girl from her mother. I would stand up in Papa's church and recite it dramatically.

She stood at the bar of justice
A creature worn and wild.
She was too young for a woman
And yet too old for a child.

They had arrested her for stealing a loaf of bread.

"Your name!" said the judge as he eyed her,
"It's Mary McGuire, if you please, sir."
"Your age!"
             "I've turned sixteen."

"Well, Mary . . ." a pen from a paper,
He gravely and slowly read,
"You are charged here, I'm sorry to say,
For stealing a loaf of bread."

Then the girl answered:

"I'll tell you just how it was, sir.
My mother and father are dead.
My little sisters and brothers
Were hungry and asked me for bread."

That was her plea; she really didn't call herself stealing when her little sisters and brothers were hungry. The hearts of everybody in the courtroom went out to her.

Every man in the courtroom,
Graybeard and dauntless youth,
Knew as she spoke to them
That she was telling the truth.

Out from their pockets came kerchiefs
And out from their eyes came tears,
And out from their faded wallets
Came treasures hoarded for years.

That was a long poem, but I could say that thing. I would dramatize it as I recited it. Then I would strut off the stage.

My father had a church at White Oak Springs and one where we were living. The one at White Oak Springs was about six miles from the White Oak Springs general store. That was really all there was to the place. The members of that church were the ones who picked us up at the train station when we moved down from Birmingham. Papa had a member there whose name was Portia, who had two sons. One was a mulatto, and the other was black. The mulatto son's father sent him to Tuskegee to go to school, but he took TB and died. Portia worked for the white man who ran a country store, who was the father of that son, and lived in the backyard of his house.

Papa knew their relationship and talked to him about how they shouldn't be living like that. The man said, "Well, I love her and I can't marry her, and I'm not married. I don't have anything to do with the government not letting me marry Portia." Papa came back home and told Mama and said, "I just don't know what to say about it. I know it's wrong, because the Bible says so, but here's a man that says he loves a woman and would marry her except that the law won't allow it. So he's doing the next best thing. I just don't know."

Mama said, "Just leave it alone and pray over it. You told him what you thought was right. Now let the Lord work it out."

Miss Portia died before Papa stopped pastoring there. That man's store was the only one within fifteen miles, so he had a lot of customers, white and black. When Portia died, he married a white woman. Before he died, he set up Portia's black son in business in Eufala.

Bought him a house and set him up as the taxi driver in Eufala with a nice car.

The same church had another member, a beautiful woman who was named Bishop. Every time I went there with Papa, she would be in bed, because she was an invalid. She had long, pretty black hair, and she was a pretty brown color. Just from her hips on down, she was invalid. She had children too. They had a tale out on her. They said she was such an attractive woman that every minister who went to their church fell in love with her. The ministers' wives would tell each other about it, and warn each other about her. One minister's wife who believed in witchcraft said, "She'll never get my husband." In the Methodist church, they rotate the pastors every two or three years, so when he went there as a pastor, that Mrs. Bishop got in there behind him. Whenever that pastor went to the town, he stayed with the pretty lady and her husband. The husband was one of the stewards of the church and always knew how much money came in. The wife would always get it from the preacher. He'd get his little salary, and she got the rest, in fact *all* of it sometimes. The old wives said the minister's wife fixed her so she wouldn't be bothering any other ministers, and that's why she was paralyzed from the waist down.

On Sundays, when church time came, people from all around would come in their wagons to worship. That same Miss Fanny Ransom who was such a good dancer, sang in the choir with a beautiful alto voice. Also one of the ladies who had the watermelons that Albert swiped, she sang in the choir. They had a choir full of people, and they did note singing. One man was the leader of the choir, and he would lead them in going over the notes first. They called them square notes. Then they would get their tune and would start singing the words to the song.

You could hear their voices ringing all through the trees and the woods, and you'd know church was going on, and you started running to get there and be a part of it. Especially the hymns. One lady there who wasn't in the choir but sat in one of the amen corners was kind of a drunk, and she had a high soprano voice. You could hear her above the others, and the more juice she drank, the higher her voice got. She got it from the moonshiners. At first I didn't know about it, because old people didn't tell us children about things like that. But I got it from one of the big girls, and then I smelled it one day, but I didn't tell Mama. You didn't tell your parents that you knew about things like that, because if you did, they'd make you go away when they got ready to talk, figuring you'd carry what they said to somebody else.

I remember my sister Beatrice got into trouble for that one time. A neighbor lady went to visit relatives and had a pig. She lived by herself and carried some sweet potatoes over to Mama's and asked if she would feed the pig some sweet potatoes and give it some water every day while she was gone for a couple of days. Mama said she'd be glad to, so the lady left the potatoes out on the little stoop at the back. The next day Mama went to get the potatoes to feed the pig the next day, and there were no more potatoes. So she came back home and in the presence of Beatrice was telling another neighbor about how the potatoes were gone. She said, "I believe Sister So-and-So got them, because she came by and she had a package under her arm." They knew she would take things. Beatrice was sitting out there playing. A couple of days later, the lady Mama accused of taking the potatoes came by and asked Mama, "How're you doing, Sister Webb?" Mama said, "Doing pretty good." The lady said, "Has So-and-So come back yet?" and Mama said, "No, she hasn't come back yet, but somebody stole the food she left me to give her pig, and I had to get something else to feed it." The lady said, "They did? Do you know who stole it?"

Before Mama could get the word out, Beatrice said, "Mama said you did." Mama was so mad at Beatrice and so ashamed; she told Papa she was going to whip her, but Papa said, "You know you ought not to have said it in front of her." So I learned not to tell things that old people did, even one time one of Papa's friends. One of his minister friends reached out at me. I went with Papa to a meeting to represent our church. Papa wasn't my pastor then; he was pastor of some other churches. I was filling out a little bit as a girl, and the minister of our church of Mount Zion reached at me and I hollered. I said, "You better not touch me, or I'll tell Mama." He said, "I was just playing. Please don't tell your Mama. I didn't mean to hurt you." I wasn't going to tell, because I knew Mama wasn't going to let me go anywhere with him. I felt I could protect myself. I could sense things, and I figured that if he had put his hands on me like I figured he was going to do, I would have hit him just as hard as I could. That was one thing that Mama taught us.

One time the two churches in our neighborhood came together and were having a big camp meeting at one of the churches. They'd have tables all around, barrels of lemonade, a lot of preaching and singing. Mama ordered a barrel of fresh fish, and a dark cloud came up. Looked like the bottom was going to drop out, and Mama was so worried, because they had paid something like forty dollars for that fish. She could see that they would lose their money because nobody would come to the meeting. But people came in horses and wagons and walked, and they were there by the hundreds.

They did have a cloudburst, and people were all packed up in the church and in people's houses around it. Some of them waited in their buggies with tops on them. After the rain poured down for awhile, it stopped. People got out and played ball; they ate all the fish including the fish heads in gravy. Mama had prayed and asked God not to let it rain, but he did and blessed her right on. "Don't tell me how to do it! You should have prayed and asked me to let you sell that fish. Telling me not to let it rain!"

We didn't have fish often, because we couldn't afford it, but we'd have it for big holidays. On the Fourth of July we would go mudding. There was a lake down there with fish in it. Part of the water ran off in a little creek. They would go down there and dam that little creek and get hoes and drag up and down the bottom of the lake. The water would get real muddy, and the fish would swim to the top. With a net they would catch the fish, and we would clean them and fry them right there. The best eating fish—fresh catfish, fresh bream! We would eat fish and have lemonade. We didn't have any ice, but we would get springwater, and the barrel we made the lemonade in would be sweating from the coolness of the water itself.

We also celebrated the twenty-eighth of May for Emancipation, because we didn't know anything about the first of January, which is the real anniversary. Mama said that when their people knew about it, it was on the twenty-eighth of May, because the white people didn't tell them for a long time so they would stay on and work. So Emancipation Day was a great big joint picnic for people from all around. People from all over would come. They would play baseball, and the moonshiners would be out there on the edge of the field with the moonshine in water buckets. They'd sell it by the dipperful. Some people would get drunk, but that was all right too, because nobody got hurt from it. The ladies were busy selling candy or pies, and a lot of the food was free. There was a lot of courting going on, walking up and down the road. One time a man came who had a car. He'd ride you a mile for a dime. The boys were treating the girls to a ride in the car. I wanted to get in a car so bad, but I was too little. There wasn't anybody who was going to pay a dime to give me a ride.

Nobody had cars out in the country but the rich white people, and they would be sitting stiff in those cars when they rode by. Ladies would be fanning themselves and wearing wide hats, real thin, looking like a net on a wide frame. The thin netted material would go over it, and they had flowers on it and streamers. As the ladies fanned, those brims would go up and down. They wore silk Georgette blouses, real thin, and you could see the petticoats underneath. A lot of them were crocheted, with pretty ribbons going through. I wanted one of them; I wanted all the pretty things like those ladies had. When I got a chance, I'd always put on Mama's high-heel shoes and walk around the house.

At the Emancipation Day picnics they raised a lot of money, and folks drank all the liquor and played hardball, and everybody was just excited and had a good time. At night you'd hear the wagons clucking home; it was just wonderful.

CHAPTER THREE

Life on the Pat Brannon Place (1921–1925)

F inally Papa decided to move us closer to Eufala, when I was about eleven years old. He wanted us to be closer to the school. I was so glad when we moved onto Mr. Pat Brannon's place. I can see that place now, outside of Eufala, on a red clay road that bogged up when it rained. It was just a one-wagon road along a hill; if you met anybody coming the other way, you'd have to get out of the road. The hill was very steep. We lived up on another hill. You would have to come down the hill to this creek, cross it, come up another hill, and then go kind of slightly down to get to our house.

The closest house to us was up on the hill, across the road. Mrs. Molly Wasbon, who was a white lady, lived there with a younger husband and her son. She was as tacky as she could be and wanted to be a reader, a fortune-teller. She was ignorant as far as literary preparedness was concerned, couldn't read or write. But they had a lot of pretty flowers all around their house. They all called Mama "Aunt Lizzie," all the poor white people. It was a way they had of not saying "Mrs." to a respected older colored person. The Wasbons had an old piece of Ford car, but at least it was a car. We didn't have anything. Then the next house was Mrs. Ramey's, about a half mile from us. Mrs. Ramey lived there with her son Mac. They were black, and Mrs. Ramey was a good friend of Mama's.

Our house sat down, kind of in a bottom, surrounded by swamps. You came down off the main road, along a little narrow private road with trees all along it, kind of muddy, and then you'd come into the opening, and there was our house. There were a lot of bushes around the house. A well sat out in the front yard, and we were so glad about the well, because we wouldn't have to carry water from the spring.

Come to think about it, I guess you'd call that house a tar-paper house. It was covered in tar paper, just the plain old black kind, over most of it, with some bare spots. The other part of it was wood. It was not a beautiful-looking place at all, and it had a front porch going clean across the front of it, that wasn't so stationary, but it would support you. On each end of it, the flooring was kind of broken out, but there was about a third of it unbroken, coming from the doors out to the ground. That's where I swept the trash on Papa. Mr. Pat Brannon lived in town but used to come to our house. He was an older man and would always be walking. Mr. Brannon was kind of slow walking, and he looked like he was as poor as an old turkey hen, but he owned a lot of land. He didn't impress me as being either intelligent or a moron. I guess it was just a nice walk for him to come out and see us. That house leaked everywhere; he really should have fixed it.

When you walked in the front door of the house, there were two rooms on the right. The first one was the kitchen. That was really the back of the house, because the front had been built to face the main road, but the trees and bushes had grown up and blocked it. So we came in from the other side, on that little private road, and used the back door as the front. Right behind the kitchen was a bedroom where Mama and Papa slept. On the left, as you came in the door, there were three bedrooms. One was a little old room just big enough to get a bed in it and a chair. I think the boys must have had that room.

We had some plum trees on the edge of the yard, and there were an apple tree and a peach tree. They hadn't been attended to for a long time, so the peaches were wormy, but Mama started putting fertilizer on them and tin in the ground around them, tending them. The next year the peaches weren't as wormy.

You walked out of the yard and about fifty feet from the yard, the hill started, not a steep hill, kind of a slope going up. We planted cotton there. To the right of the little side road that ran in front of the house, you would go up a path. The little road came in from the left side of the house. The path went up the hill past Miss Molly Wasbon's house, to Mama's good friends, the Rameys. From then on, as you went into town, there were nice houses and things all along the road. We were kind of isolated to ourselves.

This was poor land that we moved to, with a lot of rocks in the soil. They call those rocks sandstone, I guess, and people are making houses out of it now. Sometimes in plowing, you would knock up against a rock. It was hard plowing on that land, and the soil was poor.

The path we used to go to the field, you could also use to go up a high hill. You would have to cross a creek to get to that hill, and climb the hill and get up to what they called the Wide Road. That was about five miles. That road led to Clayton, Alabama. Over that hill lived a poor white family that was very friendly. My brother played with some of their boys, and they would come to our house. They would eat with us sometimes, and we would eat with them too. Any time that lady had something extra, she would give Mama some. She was a pretty lady too, didn't look real poor and crackery like some of them. I think she must have come from a right nice family. She could read and write.

We had more white neighbors than we did black ones, but it didn't make any difference to us. Mama would be gracious to them, giving and sharing. Sometimes we children would get mad because we didn't think she should be giving things away, but those people would always share with her too. We didn't say anything then.

There was another poor white family who couldn't read or write at all, and Mama wrote their letters for them. Mrs. Wasbon couldn't read or write either. This other lady would come over to the house and eat with us and everything. The funny thing about it was that a lot of black people were having a pretty hard time as far as the Ku Klux Klan and all that was concerned, but we never were bothered by them. She always told Mama, "Lizzie, you don't have to worry about a thing. We're white folks, and ain't no white folks going to bother you." This lady was *really* poor; they didn't have anything but a mattress to sleep on. But because of her race, she felt she was still a little better than we were, which was okay. We didn't think anything about it.

By that time we had nearly come down to the water's edge as far as poverty was concerned, but we were proud. It was the times, and then Mama wasn't able to get any work in town at first, and we'd have to live on what little Papa could do. Sometimes he'd come home with some sour syrup, and Mama would cook it over, or an old hen that had stopped laying. People paid him off in commodities rather than money—they didn't have any money. They seemed to get the worst of what they had, to give to the preacher. One of them said, "Mama tried to give it to somebody, and Daddy tried to give it to somebody, but they didn't want it, so we decided to give it to y'all."

Gradually things got better, and Mama was able to get some work in Eufala, doing washing and ironing for people. One day she told my brother Jim and me to stop by at a white lady's house to pick up a bundle of clothes. Jim and I thought of ourselves as the preacher's children, and we weren't going to walk through the streets carrying any clothes on our heads. We told Mama we were ashamed. I never will forget that; I can almost feel the pain now. In a quiet voice Mama said, "Come here," and put us right down beside her. She said, "I'm going to tell you something. Your father doesn't make much money. You all need clothes, and you need things like other children. I thought if I did some washing that I could help supplement your Daddy's income so that you all could look like the other children. It's no disgrace to work. It's an honor to make an honest dollar. Even if it's going around picking up cow tracks, it's better than stealing."

My brother and I wept. Mama could really tan you when she gave you a whipping, but that was worse than any whipping I ever got. It was almost sundown, but we jumped up from there and tore out down that hill and across that creek on those rocks, up the hill and to that lady's house and got those clothes. From then on, we strutted like those clothes were crowns on our heads.

That helped me after I stopped teaching school, when I had to go into domestic work. I wasn't changed. I was hungry and needed a job, and I took what I had and survived. It was a lesson I never did forget. I taught it to my one son, and when I teach Sunday school, I teach it to the children. When I taught in the public schools I told those children, "Learn to use your hands. If you're going to sweep the floor, be the best floor sweeper that they have. Whatever you do, do the best you can with it."

Then Mama started working for a lady named Mrs. Calton who had a contract to make the hot lunches at the white high school, which was right close to us. We had to pass it going to our school. They didn't have a regular hot lunch program at that time, but they did have a kitchen and a dining area. It wasn't subsidized by the county or the state, but that school in particular gave Mrs. Calton a contract to make lunches. She was skilled, and of course she had Mama with her to do the cooking. She saved every scrap; she was very conservative. All the bread crusts were pudding material. There was nothing wasted. The food that came back on the plates turned into a cup of soup. Every now and then she'd give Mama a slew of stuff at the end of the week when there wasn't any way to save it over and make something else out of it. Mama would come home loaded then.

Whenever people in Eufala got ready to have a big bash, they would try to get hold of Mama to do the cooking—big weddings, whatever. I often wondered how come the food at home didn't taste like that. I didn't have sense enough to know that Mama didn't have that kind of ingredients to put in the food, all that butter and cream. She used to make candied carrots, or carrots in white sauce for those people. She could take a cookbook and then use her own ingenuity and imagination and invent wonderful things. Whatever she did, she did with a love for doing it well and put her imagination in it. She wanted her work to look good, taste good, and last long. She believed in quality. So people would borrow Mama from Mrs. Calton.

Mrs. Calton had a lot of girls, and she had a hard time getting by, with that big family. She would sell her girls' old clothes to Mama for a little bit of money, and Mama would make them over for us. With her work at the school, Mrs. Calton made it, and got all those daughters married off to good, well-to-do husbands in big weddings. Mama did all the cooking and catering for those weddings, and she enjoyed it. We would go over and lick some of the cake pans and get some of the crusts off the sandwiches. And Mama would bring a heap of leftovers home.

At Mrs. Calton's, Mama did the cooking and the washing and the

ironing. At that time, people used a lot of starch in their clothes, petticoats and pillow slips and everything. We had to heat our irons in the
fireplace. I can see those clothes now, not a smudge or a cat face. Those
things were smooth as the paper you write on.

We children got little jobs sweeping yards for people. My first job
was for a lady whose house I'd go to after school and wash dishes and
clean up the kitchen. Then I'd go home. One day she asked me if I
knew how to cook a hen. I said, "Yes, ma'am." She had a hen already
dressed, so I put it in the pot to boil. When she came back, I was ready
to go home. She asked if the chicken was done, and I said just about.
When I got home, about an hour later, Mama came home from work
and had that chicken. The lady had called where Mama was working
and told her to come by there, because the chicken's craw was still in it.
Well, I didn't know, because she had said it was clean. She wouldn't eat
it, so she gave it to Mama. It tasted just fine, and we tore that thing up.

All this time, Albert was just in and out. He was going with a girl
named Eva May Cooley, nice looking and his age. One day he went
there and Eva May wasn't at home. Her mother said, "Albert, I haven't
turned Eva May out yet, so you must be coming to see me." "Turning
someone out" meant letting her go out with boys. That flattered that
eighteen-year-old boy. She was a wonderful cook and had a good figure. So he just fell for that. I came from school one day, and he had
married Mrs. Cooley. I said she must have conjured him, and Mama
said, "Oh, she conjured him, all right, just the way he wanted to be
conjured." I was so disgusted that I wouldn't even walk to school by
that house. I didn't want to have to speak to her.

Mr. Pat Brannon came to our house one day. That woman had sent a
shoe box of food out by Albert, full of fried fish and biscuits. It smelled
so good that we couldn't wait to eat it, but at the same time we were
afraid we would be conjured if we ate any. When Mr. Pat Brannon
arrived, Mama said, "We're fixing to put dinner on the table. Will you
have some?" He said, "Yeah, Lizzie, I'm hungry." She got that box and
gave him the food. He ate like I don't know what. We were eating our
ordinary stuff, but he was eating that stuff that Eva had sent out for us.
Didn't look like there was anything wrong with it.

Albert stayed with Mrs. Cooley for about a year and a half, but then he started drifting away. Then he got hung up with the lady across the road from us, and they claimed they got married. But Mrs. Cooley never gave up. She said she never gave him a divorce. Years after when she died, she died in the name of Eva Webb. Then we found out that she wasn't any Webb, because she was never divorced from her children's daddy. It's hard to know what she was.

Right across the street from us was a woman whose little boy went to school with me across the creek—Edward Cochran. His mama was a smart, very cunning woman. Albert married her. They lived together for awhile, but Lily Mae had a shrewd head too. He couldn't con her too much, because she'd turn around and re-con him. One time Mama had to go to town and get some groceries, and Lily Mae had to go too. It was late in the afternoon, and they were walking together. They had to go through some woods, but Lily Mae said, "I've got a gun. I carry my pistol, so if anybody bothers us, I'll blow their heads off." They went across the creek and over the hill, where there was a nice store in a kind of blue-collar neighborhood. The people who ran the store were just as crackerish as they could be, great big fat young woman and a big husband. They talked bad English, but they were good-hearted folks. On the way back home, Albert got in the bushes and jumped out and scared the fire out of them. She forgot all about that pistol and ran off and left Mama.

Eventually Albert left Lily Mae and went down to Geneva and got hung up with another lady. She moved to South Carolina, and he went with her. He worked in the logging business. After two or three years, he scooted out away from her and went back to Eufala and met the wife that he died with, Irene. She had never been married, but she had a bunch of children. Her mama had never been married before her. She was good looking and very fair. He married this woman, and they had three children. She is one of the nicest, sweetest persons you ever met. But both of them used to drink liquor and get on that truck he had, go out and drink all night together. But she turned out to be a good Christian woman and a good wife for Albert. He passed in March 1985. I have heard old folks say that when the sap goes up or the sap goes down, if you have anything wrong with you, you will go at those times. I have also noticed that it's often near a person's birthday when they pass. Albert was born in February.

Mama got pregnant again when I was about fourteen. Papa was still living then. She had gone to the field and worked that morning and come back home and washed on a rub board, and somehow she must have injured her stomach. That night we were supposed to go to Silas Green. I had never gone to a Silas Green Circus in my life, and I was excited! Mama had decided to let us go. Papa was away at one of his churches. We had about fifty cents apiece, from scraping yards and sweeping yards and peddling brooms. But Mama got sick before we left. She was in so much pain, but the old midwife Aunt Charity was with her. Aunt Charity sat around making dirt dauber tea, while Mama was just having fits and spasms. I could hear Mama, and I was the oldest one at home then, so I went up to the house and went to the door of Mama's room and knocked. "What do you want?" asked old Aunt Charity.

I said, "I want to see what's wrong with my mother. I'm going to get Mrs. Ramey so Mr. Ramey can go get a doctor. My Mama's *sick*." Old Aunt Charity was just making dirt dauber tea, out of those birds' houses. That was supposed to bring the baby, but the baby was dead. We didn't know that.

I ran up the hill to Mrs. Ramey's house, and she and her husband came. He jumped on his mule and went to town to find Dr. Salter, a young doctor, just come to town. When Mr. Ramey got to Eufala, which was very small at that time, about five thousand people, he found Papa there and told him about Mama. Papa was supposed to have been going to his church, but I guess he had stopped to see the Silas Green show. Mr. Ramey found Dr. Salter, and they came out there over some bad roads. I don't know how he made it, but he got there.

He said, "What are you doing, old lady?"

Aunt Charity said, "I'm just making this tea."

He told her, "Get me some hot water." I heard Mama hollering. In the meantime, Papa had come home and tore in there. The doctor didn't know he was Mama's husband, and he said, "Old man—"

Papa said, "That's my wife."

The doctor said, "You can stay if you want, but I'm not going to have any hanky-panky around here. You just get on out. I don't want anybody in my way. I'm liable to lose her; she's hemorrhaging." He took the forceps and pulled that baby out of Mama, because she couldn't have had it. You could see the marks on the baby's head where the forceps had been. Lord, have mercy! That really scared me. I said I'd never have a baby as long as I lived. And wasn't it a shame that the men couldn't have a baby too! Women had to go through all that hurting.

I had to wash all those bloody rags and quilts that Aunt Charity had gathered. The blood had gone through everything, the sheets and the mattress. We did have a well, thank God, so I could draw the water from the well, but it took a lot of washing.

Mama got pregnant again right after that. We were kind of disgusted with Mama, wondering when she was going to stop having babies. We had hated it about the baby that died, and we had named him Freeman and buried him up on the hill. When the new baby came, Mama called me to her bed. The baby looked just like the one that died. I was the oldest one at home, and she was going to let me name him. I was so excited. I named him Frank after my Aunt Sister, who I had wanted to go stay with when I was younger. She had married a man named Tanks, so I named the baby Frank Tank. It's a silly name, but Mama let it stay. He never did use the Tank part, called himself Frank T. Mama was nineteen when Beatrice was born, so she was somewhere near forty when Frank T. was born. He was a baby when Papa died.

He grew up petted and spoiled. He could get by with anything. Lazy! Good brain. He could remember anything, but he was just lazy. Lib nursed him, and everybody said she helped spoil him. Everybody said she wore two rockers down, rocking Frank T. Finally he grew up and joined the service when the war came along, but he never finished high school. All four of my brothers went in the service in World War II.

My father was a circuit minister, and he believed the word of God and the doctrines of the church. He helped everybody to it, especially the ministers. As a result, he wasn't so well liked by some of them who did unorthodox things as ministers. A lot of good appointments that he deserved, he didn't get because they kind of blackballed him.

One time the bishop had gotten with the presiding elders, who in the Methodist church recommend the promotion of ministers. They didn't give Papa such a good report, saying they ought to keep Webb out of this deal that they were going to make. They came up with a secret plan that was wrong for the church, and they were going to carry it through during the annual conference.

Back then, people printed handbills on rough sheets of paper and passed them around. Papa got someone to print some of these up for him, entitled "Billy's Dream." Billy dreamed that the bishop and these folks had got together and were going to do so and so during the annual conference—predicting that plan. When Papa had these scattered around the congregation and among some of the other churches, the plan was ruined. They couldn't put it through.

They wondered who had given away their scheme. Now, Papa's name was Willie—Willis James Webb—but they thought Webb was not smart enough to do it, and they never caught on. I must have got a lot of my cunning from my daddy.

Papa was a smart man, but he never tried to take advantage of his congregation. He was a carpenter too, and a brickmason, and he would earn extra money building chimneys for people's houses. I bet he didn't get five dollars a chimney, and that was from the ground up. He was always going around trying to get extra work to supplement his salary.

One year we had laid our little crop by and had done well. We had two bales of cotton, and Papa was taking it to town to sell so we could buy winter clothes. Two bales of cotton would have been worth about a hundred dollars. Mama got sick and couldn't go with him, so he took the mule and wagon by himself and went to Clayton, where they were getting a good price for cotton.

In the meantime, every year the Methodist ministers would carry what they called "dollar money" to the conference. That was a dollar for every member in their congregation, and the money was all put in a general fund for ministers' widows, foreign missions, and so on. Each minister was to go to the conference, make his report, and contribute his dollar money. Papa had forty dollars that he had gotten from his three churches, and he had it on him when he went to do his cotton business.

He got to Clayton, got his cotton money, and we heard the cluck-cluck-cluck of the wagon as he came home. You could hear that wagon from two miles away, rolling along that road. We tore out to meet him, because we were so excited about having some new shoes and cloth to make our dresses and pants and shirts for school. Maybe there would even be some cheese or some fresh meat. There Papa was with not a thing for us. Talk about a dark judgment day for us! If Mama had had high blood pressure, she would have had a stroke. Papa had lost every penny.

He had stopped at a minister's home in Clayton to use the outside johny. A black person couldn't use any public bathrooms in the town. When he pulled down his pants, the money must have slipped out in his little sack that he carried it in, because when he left that minister's house he went back downtown to buy the things for us, and he found that he didn't have his sack.

I have never seen my daddy so dejected. Here were all his children, so proud that they had worked hard in the field all year and the crop had turned out well. Mama was just smiling to think that she would be sewing some new clothes for us. She was lucky; she was the only one around that had a sewing machine. He had lost the dollar money and lost the money we had all worked for all year. Everything got quiet, and then I heard Mama crying. But she brushed herself up later on and came out and said, "Well, your daddy had some misfortune and lost the money. But we are going to do something."

We had a crib full of corn, too, and we went out there the next day and started shucking and shelling corn to sell to get his dollar money. If Papa hadn't had that dollar money, he wouldn't have had any church to go to. We sold almost all of our corn to make up that money. I can't recall how we managed after that, but we went to school and survived it somehow. We had two cows and a calf, and they did sell the calf. That must be how they got enough to get by.

Another time, Papa was sure he was going to get a better church, and he went to conference on the train, all excited. He had had a fight with one of his officers. The sisters had got together and raised seventy-five dollars to buy him a suit. He was such a big man that he had to order his clothes.

But the officers of the church said they needed the money for repairs and told the sisters not to give it to Papa. This particular officer was a blacksmith, and the sisters had given the money to him. Papa went to the blacksmith's shop and asked him for the money. The blacksmith said, "I'm not going to give you anything."

Papa said, "Why? They raised this money for my suit." He didn't have any clothes except an old, patched-up suit, but as a minister he was supposed to look dignified. Papa and the blacksmith got into a fight, and the smith hit Papa. Papa grabbed him and fell on top of him and broke his rib, but he got the seventy-five dollars and got his suit.

All the children started taunting us about that, saying, "Your daddy got in a fight! The preacher got into a fight!" I was ashamed at first, but after awhile I started saying, "Yeah, and he ought to have killed him. A preacher is just like anybody else when somebody tries to take advantage of him. I wish I had been there; I would have hit him too."

When time for the annual Methodist conference came, they would give the pastors their appointments for the year. It seemed that they would always be transferring our father from one church to another. It was hard for us as children to move from a community where we had made friends and learned to feel at home. We were always apprehensive at that time of year, wondering whether or not they were going to let Papa come back or send him somewhere else. Oftentimes Mama didn't move with him but just stayed where she was. The churches were so small that they couldn't take care of a pastor's family. There wasn't anywhere for us to stay anyway, so we stayed put. Papa would commute back and forth home.

We had an old mule, and Papa would leave Saturday on the mule to go to one of his churches. He would tend to church business on Saturday with the members and then stay on for the services on Sunday. So many times, after the worship service, the people would all go home, and nobody invited him to dinner. There he was, way away from home.

One time there was a member who always said, "Reverend, I want you to come and have dinner with my family." But she had a lot of children, and he didn't want to take food away from them, so he excused himself. She kept asking, until one Sunday he decided to accept. When he got to the house, one child went in one direction, and another child went in another direction. He waited and waited for her to call him to dinner. Finally she did, and on the table was one fried egg, a hoecake of cornbread, and some milk. He cut half of the egg and ate it, and, knowing they didn't have much, said he just couldn't eat any more. She smiled and said, "Reverend, if I had known you liked egg that much, I would have cooked more."

Another time he went to one of his members' house, and he was very hungry. She fixed some food—it wasn't much—and he ate it all. She had children too, and he could just see her expression going down as she thought, "Here this man has eaten up all the food." That time he had some money, and there was a little store not far down the road. He said, "Sister So-and-So, take this and go and buy some food for the children." She was so happy, because the food he had eaten was probably all she had, and now with the money, she could buy much more than that.

He told us, "I want you all to know this: any time that you see a minister and you think he is hungry, no matter how bad a minister he might be, make him welcome to your food." I have kept that up in my life.

If we needed the mule for plowing, Papa would walk. He would carry his old leather grip with a shirt in it and a handkerchief made out of a piece of flour sack that Mama had hemstitched around to make it look nice. His shirt would be starched with cornmeal starch. Mama would put some meal in the water and just boil it and drain off the water to get the starch. Most of the shirts didn't have collars on them, because the men wore celluloid collars. It was a good thing that Papa wore a coat, because sometimes the shirts would be all patched up under the coat where you couldn't see the patches. Sometimes he would only wear a shirt front, and then he would preach flat-footed, not moving around or using his arms. I would be so proud—I knew my daddy was the preachingest man that ever was. We thought he could beat anybody in the world.

One time we were plowing together on this Pat Brannon place. Papa was plowing the horse and I was plowing the cow. I think we were planting cotton. Somehow or other the plow got away from me; I couldn't hold it. He kind of hollered at me.

I stopped that cow right there, and I looked at him. I said, "Do you know I'm doing a boy's job?" My oldest sister was frightened of Papa. He could scare her and all the rest of them, but I would stand up to him.

He said, "Don't you talk to me like that."

I said, "Well, I'm telling you the truth." So he didn't bother me.

One day he decided he was going to get me. Mama had gone to visit her sister up in Fort Mitchell, Alabama. At that time Beatrice was off at school, so I was the big girl in the house. Papa told us to hurry up and get ready to go to the field. Lib was standing in the door, ready to jump if he said jump. "Come on, Sarah, we're going to the field!"

I had finished cooking breakfast and was sweeping out the kitchen and the back porch. I was just about through, and I said, "Yes sir, Papa, as soon as I get through sweeping out the porch."

He said, "I said, come on, *now!*"

I didn't stop. "Yes sir, Papa, just as soon as I get through." Lib was just drawing up, waiting for him to hit me. He was standing outside, and with my last swoop I swept that trash right off on him, *swish!* It looked like Papa just went up in smoke. Lib like to have fainted! She was big by that time, and she said she like to have *fainted* because she knew Papa was going to kill me.

When all that trash cleared, I could see Papa, just busting out laughing and calling me crazy. He said, "If you weren't so much like me, I'd kill you."

I must have been a little like my father, but I took after my mother too. I always wanted to be like Mama. She was a great public speaker and used to help my father with his sermons.

At Pat Brannon's place, we started going to school in town, three miles away in Eufala. We stayed up on a little hill, and we walked down this hill to a little creek and then up another hill and hit the city limits. Other children used to laugh at us and say we lived plumb out of town and nearly out of the country. It didn't bother me; I determined in my heart that I was going to make those children regret what they said.

I decided I was going to make those children stop grinning about what I didn't have and make them look up to me for something. I knew I was pretty good in school, so I was going to really study. I have gotten down on the floor at night with a lot of lightwood knots, fat stuff, for light, on my belly on the floor and studied my lesson. Got it too. We had a woman principal named Mrs. Elmira Jackson, who was a very fair person. The school started at the first grade and went through the ninth grade. Any time any of the teachers was absent, I was the subteacher. That's how smart I was, and how my principal treated me. And I'll tell you, I had order, too, buddy. The ones that misbehaved, I'd send to her. I didn't whip anybody, but they didn't want to go to Miss Elmira, either.

When we first started school in Eufala, I only had two dresses. One I would wear to church and Sunday school. I was secretary of the Sunday school. Monday I wore that dress to school until Friday. I had some work clothes, raggedy things that I wore around the house, because I would put off my dress when I'd come from school and hang it up. Then Friday, I'd put on the other dress, which was fresh, and wear it Friday. And then Sunday I wore it. I still was very proud.

Some of the girls in my class were good dressers. At that time they were wearing sandals and different colored silk stockings, half stockings, and silk pongee dresses. In the meantime, Mama got some work in town, and we started getting a little more clothes. The people she worked for would give her clothes, and she'd make them over for us. My Aunt Sister had moved up north, and she'd send us boxes of clothes once a year. Mama would get in there and start fixing those for us, and we started dressing better.

When I came into my womanhood, I had always said I wouldn't, because I had seen my sisters' clothing, and I said that would never happen to me. Mama insisted that it would, as I got older, but I was determined that it would never happen. I didn't know that this was the routine for women. When it did happen to me, I was down on my knees saying my prayers, and Mama spotted it and said, "Sarah." She had a voice that told you whatever you wanted to know. The way she spoke, you knew it was something special, whether gloomy special or joyful special, it was the tone of her voice. Looked like something dropped in me; I knew she had something special to tell me about, and I didn't want to hear it. Then she told me all about the facts of life. I had heard about them from the big girls, but they had told me entirely wrong. Because they knew I was young and foolish, they had some fun with me. Mama said, "Don't let a boy kiss you; don't let a boy touch you. If he does, you might get weak and get pregnant and disgrace your family." She didn't spell it out in detail, but she said enough. I thought if a boy touched me or kissed me, I could get pregnant from it. I wasn't *about* to disgrace my family. Every time a guy tried to kiss me, I'd hit him or throw a rock at him. They called me crazy. But I was just scared I would get pregnant. Later on when I grew up, I came to understand what Mama meant, that the touching brings on something else.

When I came into womanhood, I cried all night. Mama showed me how to fold across the little diaper cloths you used. They didn't have any Kotex or anything like that. We used old cloths from your brothers' or your father's shirttails, and we had a bag to put them in, and then we'd have to wash them out. When you were in that state, you couldn't get your feet wet or wash your hair. You couldn't bathe until that was over.

Our Sunday school teacher was a handsome young man. He grabbed me one day and kissed me, and I felt funny. I knew that wasn't right; it wasn't the way you'd kiss a child. I was thirteen or fourteen then. Finally he proposed that I go with him. He had a wife too, and I knew that was wrong. I said, "Mr. Brown, that's wrong." But he told me he loved me and was going to give me some money. I thought about it and decided that if I got that money, I could tell Mama that I found it and we could buy food with it.

He was supposed to meet me down in the woods between our house and the church, to give me the money. What I did was get all my sisters and brothers to play hide-and-seek so I could go hide in the woods and meet Mr. Brown. But when it came time, the fear of the devil got in me. I got so frightened that I didn't go down where I was supposed to meet him. I got so scared that I could see babies; I feared I would disgrace my mama. At that age, I thought that if a man touched you, you could get pregnant.

Mr. Brown worked in one of the leading stores downtown. You would see him out washing the windows or cleaning up around the store, and I had to pass that store to get to school. He was standing there the next day, and he said, "What happened last night?" I said some kind of lie about how I saw a ghost and was afraid. He said, "I still have the money for you." I said, "Mr. Brown, if you don't leave me alone, I'm going to tell Mama. You are a man, and I am a girl, and you have a wife too. Don't ever say anything like that to me, please sir." He didn't.

In the meantime, Jesse Corbett still loved me and pursued me from Wilsonville to Eufala. He was around Albert's age and had a job. He gave me a beautiful ring that was supposed to be my engagement ring. To keep him from bothering me, I told him I'd marry him. But there was still Mac Ramey, who was seven years my senior, waiting until I came of age, and I had told him that when I got older I would marry him.

All that was exciting for me, to have this big grown man at my feet and wanting to do anything he could to make me happy. He would come and cut wood and stumps. My brother Jim and I were the ones who were supposed to go to the woods and bring home fat pinewood stumps for the fire. We'd put it in a sack and put it across our shoulders to bring it home. Mac, bless his heart, would hear that old axe sounding over in the woods. He was strong! He would cut so much of that stumpwood, big old hunks of it, and load up their two-horse wagon and bring it to us. They ran a good-sized farm. When he got the opportunity, he would load up the wagon with oak wood and fatwood, bring it to our house and throw it in the yard. Later he would come and cut it up, just to get a chance to be around me.

We weren't allowed to take what we called "treats" from boys, although Beatrice had gotten away with those candy sticks all the time. But I wasn't supposed to take any present unless it was a birthday or something like that, because then the boy might think he was buying his way into some other things. Mac would bring me candy, but I couldn't bring it home. There was a little house in a field up from us. He would bring me candy and put it under the steps of that house, and I would go up there with my brother Jim to get it. I had to let Jim in on it so he wouldn't tell, but he ate most of it. We'd go up there and eat so much candy that I'd almost get sick.

I couldn't go anywhere at night or even in the day by myself, unless Jim went with me. The same thing was true with Beatrice and Albert. Sometimes I would have to pay Jim to get him to go with me. He would pretend he didn't want to go, and he'd say, "What you going to give me?" So he was the candy man.

There were those two older men courting me in my teenage years, and I just played with them. As I grew up and finished high school, I got out of contact with them. I saw Jesse about eight years ago, and he said he still loved me. He had been married and separated. I said, "We are too old for that now. I don't need any husband. I'm doing nicely and have my family around me. I'm not lonely. I'm very active in my church work. You are a good man, but I don't think it was meant for us to be man and wife."

By the time I was finishing high school, my father was pastoring his last church at Hartford, Alabama. My oldest brother was born in that town. Now here my brother is, just about grown, and they send Papa back to that little church. Most of the old members knew him and were happy to have him back as their pastor. Papa died in that church of a heart attack when he was fifty-three, after he had been sick for several months because of an accident at home.

We had an old cookstove, and the oven door wouldn't stay shut because the spring was broken. We would use a stick to prop it shut. Sometimes Papa and Mama would get out of bed late at night and fix a snack. It wasn't like having some crackers or opening a can of sardines. They would get greens out of the garden right by the house, and fry them, and have a little hoecake. One night Papa had gotten up, and some of us children had moved the stick so that the oven door was hanging open. In the dark, Papa bumped his leg against it and knocked the skin off. That wound got irritated, and he put home remedies on it, but it got so bad that he went to a doctor. The doctor said blood poisoning had set in and that the leg would have to come off. Papa said, "I came here with two legs, and when I die, I'm going to have two legs."

After that, Papa got asthma, and Mama had to put a mattress on the floor for him, and a chair turned upside down, with pillows propped up for him to lean on, because he couldn't breathe if he lay down. He stayed sick for a couple of months, and that was when I was sixteen and getting ready to graduate from the ninth grade, the final grade of the Eufala high school. Papa was proud of all his children, although he would get mad when Albert would run away, but the more I think about it, the more I think I really was his favorite, and he really wanted to be there for my graduation. Papa told me, "If you are the valedictorian of your class, I'll give you ten dollars." In the meantime I was saving money for my graduation dress. We used to sweep yards for people, and they'd give us a dime. Back then people didn't have grass, just bare ground and leaves and flowers. I would do other errands and chores too, and save up my money.

Papa got a little better, and he wanted to go back to his church. Mama told him he wasn't physically able and went to the doctor and asked him about it. The doctor said, "Lizzie, let him go. Let him do anything he wants to do, and he doesn't need to be worried about anything. He could drop off any minute. Whatever makes him happy, let him do it." She gave in, but she didn't go with him, because there wasn't enough money for both of them to go. It wasn't far, but he had to go on a train for seventy or eighty miles, and we couldn't afford that. I just knew that since Papa had gotten well enough to go to his church, he would be able to go to my graduation exercises when he got back. He went on down, and that Sunday morning he got up in the pulpit and preached. While he was preaching, he started passing out. They picked him up, and he was gone.

I was in secondary Sunday school that Sunday morning, and here came this crazy woman in, hollering it out, "Hey! Elder Webb is dead!! Just got the news, Elder Webb's dead!" I was just killed. My Sunday school teacher came in and got me and said, "You come on along; your Mama needs you." That foolish woman never should have come hollering in there like that. I didn't know what to do. I couldn't control Mama. Mama cried and went on, but then she straightened herself up and said, "The Lord is going to take care of us."

We buried him. I went to the funeral that day on the twenty-eighth of May, 1925. I never will forget it. That night was graduation at the high school, and I was the valedictorian. I had a long oration that I had practiced and preached on. I had said it to Papa, and he had been so proud! I had it down pat, I thought. Miss Elmira, the principal, told me I didn't have to say it, that everybody would understand because of Papa's funeral. But I was determined to say it. When I stood up to say it, I couldn't think of a word, and you could have heard a pin drop. Graduation was a great time in Eufala for black people; everybody tried to go, and the church was packed full of people. I just stood there, and after awhile, it just started pouring in like water. I opened my mouth, and the words came forth, "As I look forward to an unknown future . . ."

People gave me gifts! I had a cotton basket full of gifts. Maybe because of the death of my daddy, they felt sorry for me. Mama didn't come to the graduation exercise; she just couldn't do it. My brother Jim went with me. I thought I was the smartest person, knew everything, but there was so much I didn't know. I did know some important things, though. I knew where I wanted to go, what I wanted to be, and what I *wasn't* going to be. I knew that I was going to be somebody, because I always felt that way. It didn't matter when we didn't have food or clothes like other people.

CHAPTER FOUR

Teaching Career and Marriage (1925–1929)

B efore Papa died, he told Mama, "I have always wanted to have a home for you and the children." They had had the one early in their marriage that they bought and lost. And he had never been able to get another one. He said, "If I should die, I want you to take the insurance money and buy you all a place."

When he died, he belonged to the Masons and the Knights of Pythias and another one that was outside of Alabama, some insurance company. Often you belong to one of those insurance companies up north that doesn't even have an office in your state, and you don't ever get anything from it. We didn't get anything out of those, and Mama had to threaten to sue the lodge to get anything from them.

All the preachers came around and offered sympathy, and when they found out Papa had some insurance, they wanted to borrow some. Those lowdown scamps, some of them came and tried to pretend that Papa owed them. Mama said, "Well, I want to pay his bills." I stepped in there with her and said, "Unless they bring a note in here with Papa's signature, we ain't paying none of them nothing." Mama minded me then, even though I was only a girl. I knew that much.

But we buried Papa and had nine hundred dollars left over, which made us millionaires. Mama bought fifty-three acres with a little house on it, a house that didn't leak. It was close to town, on the north side of Eufala, and had eleven large pecan trees on it. I was so proud; nobody could tell us anything now. Papa had died in the Pat Brannon place where it rained in on us all the time, but now we had a house that didn't leak.

· The land was good, but it had a lot of hills in it. The house was on a kind of level place, slightly elevated. The land ran down in front of it to a little creek we had to cross to get to town. Behind the house was a deep gully, where we threw our trash. The boys would go down in it. Up on the hill sat our little church, the Mount Zion Church. Mama had been teaching a little private school at Mount Level, a Baptist church over to the east of Eufala and not far from our house, when I was finishing high school. After Papa died, she decided she wasn't going to teach it anymore. She was making more working at Mrs. Calton's than she was at the little private school, and it was more steady. They offered me that teaching job when I graduated, and I accepted it and worked about a month.

I had about fifteen students, all different grades, all in one room. One of the boys lived across the street from us. His name was Edward Cochran. I would carry him with me, and we would walk across the creek and up a steep hill. It almost looked like a mountain to me, and there was just a path on it. When we'd get to the top, we would cross over to another little hill, to Mount Level.

Sometimes we had a blackboard, and sometimes we didn't. Paper was something special too; any piece of paper, like a handbill, that had a clean back, I saved. I printed the ABCs on the back of it. Next to each one, I put the cursive letter. That's the way I started the primer grades. On another big sheet, I wrote the numbers 1 to 100. The children looked at these, and I used a pointer to teach them to recognize the letters and the numbers. We'd go over all the letters and say them out loud, and then I'd start having the children come up and point out an "o" or a "c" and go through them backwards.

Then I'd put "bat" on the board and draw a line under the "at" and show them how there were two words in that word. "You've got a 'bat,' and you've got an 'at.'" I'd have little words like that—"bat," "cat," "sat"—that they'd learn to spell. We had a little old primer book, and they'd begin to be able to recognize those words in the book. I'd ask them how many cats they found on a page, and how many of the other words we had learned. They'd look around and find them.

Then they learned to count, first on their hands. Then I'd say, if one was cut off, how many would you have? They'd bend down one finger and count how many were left. We'd start arithmetic that way in the primer grades.

When they got to the third grade, they could write a letter and fill out a blank to order from a catalog. I always kept a bunch of old catalogs for that. People got their things that way more than going to the store.

The fourth-graders were big people, because the children came late to school—beginning at seven or eight. But by the time my students got to the fourth grade, they knew most of the times tables. When they got to the sixth grade, they were older than I was. I was only seventeen, and some of the students were nineteen, looking down on me like I was a brat. I told them that if they didn't want to mind me, there was the door.

That was my first school, and I didn't have any teacher training or anything to work with but what I made up myself. I didn't start getting any training until I started going to Alabama State Teachers' College in Montgomery in the summers to keep up my accreditation later. So in the first years of my teaching, I just used what I had learned from observation and figured out my own ways of teaching. Even later, what I learned at Alabama State didn't surpass what I already had in my mind.

In the meantime, I took the state teachers' exam. It was given twice a year and was in two categories, Third Class and Second Class. The Second Class was more or less for people teaching in high schools. The Third Class certificate was for people who taught up to the sixth grade and sometimes the ninth, depending on how many teachers there were in your school. If you taught in a school where you had four teachers, you might teach some of the ninth-grade subjects if the school went that far.

The test consisted of current events, arithmetic, English, history, maybe geography. The test was the same for all the teachers in the state, for the same kind of certificate. There was a lot of writing done, not like the tests they give now, yes or no kind of things. You had to explain yourself. If there was a problem, you had to solve it there on the page; if there was a sentence to analyze, you had to write that sentence out and detail the parts of speech.

I passed, and it was the first time I had ever taken the exam. I was so excited that I had passed that exam and passed it like nothing flat! I said, "Great goodness alive, I'm going to be a full-blown teacher! Now I'll get a better school, a full-class state school." I wrote the Alabama superintendent of schools and applied for a school. They gave me a school in Clio, Alabama, the same place I was born. My son was born there too. Isn't that a strange thing? Went all the way around the world, and back to Clio, in a circle. I was seventeen years old when I went to take that school, and of course I lied to the school board so I could have that job. You were supposed to be twenty-one. White people just kind of look at black folks and think they all look the same, so I could pass for twenty-one with them.

Clio was just a little country town where everybody around were farmers, and it just had one main street about a block long. All the stores were on that street: the dry-goods store, the bank, the grocery store, and the post office. We had three churches for blacks: a Methodist church and two Baptist churches. We had the one black school, that went as high as the sixth grade, with two teachers. We had a cotton gin with a compress, and a mill for grinding corn. Behind the main street there was a little old jail, and that was about all.

The grocery store had big sacks of sugar. They had scales, and if you wanted a pound of sugar, they would weigh it up for you and put it in a paper bag. Same thing with meal, rice, salt. They had canned goods like sardines, and they had crackers. People from the country would come in on Saturdays and they had a porch that came out over the sidewalk, with benches where the farmers would sit on Saturday afternoon and visit relatives and friends. A lot of courting went on among the country girls and boys. They would parade up and down that street all day Saturday.

Back behind the store, there was a hitching post where folks would park their horses and mules and cows, whatever they were using for transportation. There was a watering trough back there too. Back there where the watering trough was, there was some kind of a café, like a greasy spoon, where they would sell fish sandwiches if they had fish in the town at the time, or hamburgers, which were just meat patties back then. That café was just so rough. They didn't sell liquor because it was Prohibition time, but the moonshiners were going around, and people would drink it and get in fights over jealousy, husbands going around with other women. It was a place just for blacks. You didn't go in the eating places for whites *at all*, unless you worked there or went there to the back door to get something. It didn't seem to bother the people. They were accustomed to not being served in white places; they just accepted it as a way of life.

But most of the main stores, like the grocery store, everybody shopped there. The farmers would go in there and get their groceries and charge what they needed when they were running their crop, because they didn't have money during most of the year. The man you were sharecropping for, he'd see to you getting your food and things until your crop came in. Then at the end of the year, the farmers would pay up their debts. Those store owners were tricky; everything was tricky, especially if you were a sharecropper. Sometimes the landlord ran the store, or a wife or son or daughter or son-in-law would keep the books, and you didn't argue with them at the end of the year. You had no receipt for what you got. At the end of the year they'd say, "Well, Jim, you did pretty well. You made five bales of cotton, so much corn, so many peanuts. If you had made an extra bale of cotton, you would have been out of debt." They'd do that every year.

The young men would be so despondent, the black farmers' sons. They had worked hard all year in the field, and they didn't have but one pair of shoes, and they weren't good, all torn up. At the end of the year they couldn't buy any clothes unless they went back in debt. But they would look forward to the end of the crop year, when they could buy the girls some dresses. This was the once-a-year payday for the mama, when she could get some clothes—a coat, some underwear and some shoes maybe for her children to go to school with, the short little school year they had. And how would you feel if you had to go home and tell the children, "I couldn't get the coat I promised, I can't get the shoes, I can't get the underwear"? The mama and those children had worked all year in the hot sun from sun to sun. And the landlord was getting wealthier and wealthier. His children went to school, the bus came by and picked up his children, or he carried them into town for school. They went to school a full nine months, while the farmers' children got three months. *If* they even had a school. And then they had to stop out and go in the field and work. Some of them never even learned to read and write. Then they'd get taken advantage of in the store.

And even if you had a smart one that could read and write, and he stood up and said it was so and so and so, then he was impudent. "You are saying the white person lied?" Then you were a marked sister or brother. It was hard to get ahead with that system, but some of them succeeded.

All of the white people weren't like that and didn't believe in the tyranny that some of them held over the black folks. But they had to be very careful, because they were called nigger-lovers if they were too open about how they felt.

Some of the mulatto blacks had white fathers—those men looked out for their children. And the other white men didn't bother them, because they knew they were John Smith's, or whoever's, children. John Smith would give them a little land, and he saw to them going to school. These mulattoes had to intermarry with the blacks or find another mulatto family to marry into. And that's what made it so hard for integration. The whites knew that if there was integration the children might get together and they might fall in love and marry like anybody else. And it happened that way too. The white men had been doing it all along.

There was a town called Abbeyville, Alabama, heavily populated with mulattoes. The white people built a Rosenwald school for them, because they wanted their mulatto children to have a good education. They called it a country training school, and it was better than some of the city schools. That way some of them were able to pull out of being poor. And because some of them had land, they were able to buy more. Some of them had black sisters and brothers. Their mama would marry a black man after having those white children and then have black children for him. One was just as smart mentally as the other one. They were sisters and brothers, and the light ones would help the black ones. Gradually a black middle class would form that way. Some of them really became wealthy.

On the other side of the main street in Clio, across from the dry-goods store and the grocery store and the post office, there were just a few stores that I can't remember, and houses. Most of the action was on the right side. The houses were wooden, and a few were big, beautiful ones with big front porches. There was the banker and people like that in those big houses. Then we had a white doctor, the only doctor in town. Every now and then you'd see the white ladies sometimes going shopping with their maids or with a nurse carrying their little baby. You could have someone take care of your children for three dollars a week or less. Take care of the babies, wash their clothes, stay with them at night, everything else. Those white women didn't have much to do; they had their little social clubs. They would have a cook, a housecleaner, a washerwoman coming in to wash the clothes once a week. You just knew that was the way wealthy people lived; if you were wealthy, you could have those things.

People got milk from their own cows; there weren't any dairies back then. Even the rich people would have a cow, and somebody would take care of it for them. Later on, when I went back to visit, they had gotten so they had this bottled milk with the cream on top. But the majority were milking those cows, getting that good old butter, and having buttermilk. Back then, everybody nursed their babies from the breast, but a lot of the wealthy white families would give their babies milk from the cow. Those babies stayed sick and skinny, but the little black babies grew fat, because they breast-fed them and gave them mashed-up cornbread and pot liquor, mashed-up peas. They were getting all their vitamins too, plus the milk from the mama's breast. This was before the canned baby food came out. It's a good thing that they brought that out, because those rich babies were missing a lot.

When I got to Clio, I found a place where I could room with a lady in her house. Then I settled in and got ready to begin teaching in the school. I had no more formal training for teaching than I had had in high school when the principal had me take classes when the teachers were absent. I went to Clayton, the county seat, to sign my contract, and my salary at that time was twenty-five dollars a month. Big deal. The school that I was going to was supposed to supplement that, at least fifteen dollars.

When I went to Clayton to sign my contract, they gave me a book to register the children in, with blanks that I would have to fill out each month to send to the school board before I could get my check. Nobody showed me how to fill it out, and I didn't ask anybody. I just took the book that they gave me. In that register, you were supposed to record the names and ages of your students, their parents' names, grades and attendance records. There were some sheets to be torn out, for you to put your records on and mail in to the superintendent's office, but you kept a copy in the register. In that two-teacher school in Clio, the woman who was supposed to be principal didn't know anything. The lady I roomed with worked for a white teacher who I met, and she showed me how to fill out that register. She didn't have to show me but one time, and I knew what to do. I had to even fix the thing for the lady over me, the principal. She had been teaching two or three years and had always had trouble with it; they sent it back sometimes. The next year I became principal of the school.

They used to call me Miss Nub Foot, because I wore a size four shoe and weighed ninety-eight pounds. I had students as tall as six feet and as old as nineteen years old—big, husky country girls and boys. I was afraid of them too, but I didn't let them know it. I told them that the county superintendent had sent me there because of my eligibility, and those who didn't want to be taught, there was the door. As long as I was the teacher, I was going to have order and respect. Some of them rolled their eyes. I said, "I am assuming that you're staying here because you're going to keep order. We're going to have a good time. I'm going to teach you all I know, the best I can, and love doing it. I'm looking to you to get your lessons and study and try to learn something while you're here these few months." I had one old boy one time, who came up there and had a knife and had threatened a boy on the school grounds, and I attempted to take it from him. He told me one thing and another and talked back, and I told him to leave. He said he wasn't going anywhere.

In the black neighborhoods, we used to have school trustees, men who you could call if a problem came up, and they would back you up. They could go down to the courthouse and get you fired too, if they thought you were unfit morally. A teacher had to be very careful with her conduct, because they could mess you up. So I sent for one of those trustees, and he came and got the boy. That boy couldn't read and write, and he was seventeen years old. I really felt sorry for him, because he needed to read. He came back and asked my pardon and asked if he could come back to school. I said, "Well, you go up and get one of the trustees, and we'll see what we can work out." He did, and the trustee said, "If you can tolerate him, I can. But it's going to be up to you." I said, "Well, let's give him another chance."

That's what we did, and I got that boy on my side. I said, "Now you're going to be my assistant and help me keep order on the grounds." Before that year was out, he was able to sit down and order something out of the Sears Roebuck catalog. And before that, he used to hold his book down and let the little children tell him what the words were. But he learned how to read in six months, and he came back the next year. That was my first year of teaching.

It just shows how different things were back then, that you were able to motivate children. Learning was something they didn't have. So many children were taken out and put to work on the farm before they could learn anything, that it was a privilege to go to school and learn. Education was something that was special. People who did well as farmers tried to send their weak children to school to get an education so they wouldn't have to work so hard, not realizing that if you send inferior material, that's what you're going to get back. They would try to take care of the weak ones that way and let the strong ones live by the sweat of their brow. It just doesn't work that way.

The state gave the teachers a list of the books they were supposed to study, and I would make out lists for all the grades and send them to the parents, for them to buy the books in town at the store. Most of the children couldn't get all the books, so I encouraged them to study with each other. I'd have my lesson plans in my mind, and the goals to reach for each grade. If they didn't reach the goals, they couldn't go to the next grade. That made the children anxious to keep up. I would help them all I could.

The children would be in little groups around the room, and I would go from group to group. I would ask the ones who had books to sit with the others who didn't, and read together. I taught them about sharing that way.

And I would use the little old blackboard that we had. When it came to teaching history or geography, I would do it in a storytelling way. They could visualize a story better than they could if you read the information to them. In the readers from second grade through fourth grade, they would write stories that had a moral. When you got through reading the story, you asked the children, "Now what was the moral to that story?" And they could explain.

We had a wonderful time with geography. I'd say, "You're living in a geographical place yourself. Those of you who live on farms, study about this area, your farm, the crops, what the livestock eat and cost. Those who live by the water, study about fishing for a living."

In history, we had Alabama history and United States history too. That was a kind of fascinating thing, like storytelling. I would explain to them, "Right now what we are doing is making history. You might not ever be in a book, but you are making history. History is things that happened in the past, and things that you do every day, as long as you live, that's history. The people who write our school books think the important things that children should know are written in a book, and we study that book to find out what those important things were. We learn from that, but there are also important things outside of the books. Sometimes history kind of repeats itself, so whatever happened during a period of time to people who did certain things is going to come back maybe in our time if people do enough of the same things that caused it before. We will learn from those other people that this happened to."

We would start with the revolutionary war and how it got started, the capital of Alabama, who lives there and what they do. I didn't teach them much about voting, because blacks were not voting much at that time unless they paid poll tax. That tax was around six dollars, a lot of money. You had to be very ambitious to want to vote. Sometimes they would bother you if you tried to do that; they thought you were too ambitious. They say that ignorance is bliss; well, those children and their families were just uneducated and ignorant, so they didn't care about voting. They didn't read, they didn't have any televisions, they didn't have any newspapers, no nothing. They only learned from hearsay and stories passed down from one generation to another. Sometimes if a relative came visiting from another place, they might hear about what was happening there.

I taught the children about the Indians, about the slavery business and the Civil War and Emancipation. The children were frightened of Indians, afraid they would shoot them with a bow and arrow. But I told them it was the Indians' country first and that they were just like anybody else. The only difference there was between the Indians and us was that we were brought here, and they lived here before us. They were proud people, and this was their country, and I can understand why they fought. We talked about how they fought and how they lost, and how the white people would make treaties with them and then break them. Especially we talked a lot about the Choctaw Indians and the Chickasaws, who were in Alabama, and how some of the Indians and some of the blacks really got together and intermarried.

All of the history stuff wasn't written in those books. They wrote what they thought we should know. Some of the black tribesmen over in Africa had slaves themselves, and they sold some of the people to the slave traders who brought them over here, for a strand of beads or something. But those who came over were the ones who couldn't help themselves. We were just nonviolent and nonresistant once they got us here. I'm sure that the men probably fought, but the women didn't have much choice. We talked about all that at length.

I told the children, "Although history doesn't show this, doesn't spell it out the way I am explaining it to you, some of the whites helped out with the Underground Railroad and some of the Civil War was

Sarah with pupils in Ariton, Alabama

Winterfred Murray,
Sarah's landlady in
Westbay, Florida

James David Hayes as
an army private, about
1943

Wedding picture of Sarah and Andrew A. Rice, January 1953

Rice's house, where Sarah moved
after she and Rice were married

Rice about to step aboard Charlie,
his "old piece of car," about 1953

Rice at home, 1954

Mother Dickerson (Sarah's mother), left, and Mother Telfair, Jacksonville, Florida, 1953

Sarah on the beach, Little Talbot Island, Florida, 1957

Sarah and Rice at Ellen
Hutchings's wedding,
May 1981

Sarah's sister Beatrice,
1981

Sarah, 1987

because of that. All whites aren't bad. If it hadn't been for them, we wouldn't have gotten freed, because we didn't have any weapons to fight a war with. Some of those people saw that it was wrong to have us enslaved, and they voted against it, and they were willing to fight to help us get our freedom. I'm thankful to those people. We always will have people like that."

It used to be that a person who came from Mississippi was just considered to be a bad guy. When I was coming up, people used to say that folks from Mississippi were *bad* folks. But you've got bad people in every state, and you've got good ones too. I tried to put emphasis on those things in my history teaching.

We had a pretty good time with history; I didn't have any problem. But I did have a little problem with English, because it was taught a little differently back then. It started off with the parts of speech and sentence structure. Then we used to diagram sentences. It was especially when we got to verbs and adverbs and adjectives that we had trouble. A lot of times they sound alike; it just depends on how you use them in a sentence. We didn't have any libraries for students to go look things up. I had a dictionary, and we would use it for our reference book. It's been so long ago that I've almost forgotten everything we did.

In math, I had trouble getting them to understand the decimals. They could understand the regular fractions, but when it came to the point thing, they got confused. I would start the beginners off by teaching them to count to 100. Then they would count to 100 by tens and by twenties. Then they started writing the numbers down, and after that they started the adding. I would switch the order around, so they would have to understand what they were doing and couldn't just memorize. Sometimes I would ask them to go backwards, from 100 down, or sometimes I would jump right in the middle. In the second grade, they kept working on that addition and subtraction. In the third grade we started the multiplication tables. They learned tables until they got through the fourth grade. By the end of the fourth grade, they could say all the tables. When you had learned the tables, you were ready for the multiplication of any number. You could multiply what five times two was. And then that carrying thing was another thing that I had to work pretty hard with. They couldn't understand that at first, but they learned.

I knew that some of the little beginners did better than the older students, because I caught them first. I think the hardest job is getting a child started in school. Once you get him started and get him interested in the lesson, he can slide through the rest, but if he's got a bad foundation, he's got a problem all the way through. The sixth-graders had a tough time, because they were big but often had not had good teachers and couldn't even keep up with my fourth-grade people. We just had to dig back. A lot of those older children had to stop out of school and work in the fields, and I hated that. Finally in one school, I asked the parents if the children could come to my house at night after working in the field, because they really wanted to learn and were doing pretty well and hated to drop out of school. That whole year I taught those students at night. They were tired, but they came just in their field clothes.

I wanted the children at the end of the term—because some of them weren't going to come back any more—I wanted them to be able to read and write when they left that three- or four-month school. I was determined that they should learn how to read and write and figure some. If they could get that, regardless of the history or the English, they could order something from a catalog, or they could write a letter even if the spelling was kind of bad. But I did emphasize spelling too; we had spelling matches every day. Those were my priorities when it came to my work in the classroom.

Back in those one-room schools, there wasn't any paperwork to carry to the principal's office. My only report was once a month to the county superintendent. There was a county supervisor who came visiting in the schools, and we would have a monthly teachers' meeting that lasted three or four hours. Every time I went, I would have to buy a new dress, because I was buying cheap dresses of some kind of rayon that would draw up when you washed it. I'd have my one dress, and it would eventually get dirty and have to be washed. A friend of mine told me not to be so cheap. The whole year she wore a navy blue coat suit and looked good, never changed. She said, "Buy you one good dress and wear it every time. It's better than these old cheap things. Same thing with shoes." She taught me a lesson.

In the meantime, Mama had married another minister named Elder Dickerson, who had been a good friend of my father's. He was a presiding elder, and they are next to the bishop in the AME church. They have the pastor, the presiding elder, and the bishop. The pastor has authority over his congregation, but he has to be guided by something like a constitution of the church. The presiding elders recommend to the bishop the men they want for pastors in their district. Each state is divided into districts. The presiding elder goes around quarterly and holds conferences at the churches and gets a report on how many members there are, how much money they took in, and the general condition of the church. He is able, then, to keep up with what's going on in his district. Then the bishop will have a meeting with the presiding elders to determine how things are going.

It made me mad for Mama to marry him, but I didn't have any sense. I didn't understand how hard it was for Mama to try to keep the family going by herself. When Mama got ready to marry him, she washed her one pair of stockings and hung them out on the line to dry. We had a goat that ate those stockings. Mama was so upset, but I had a pair of stockings that I let her have so she could be married in stockings.

Mama left our house and went to live on his place but didn't rent our house out. He had a small plantation of some fifty acres about six miles outside of Eufala, but he hadn't finished paying for it. He owed five or six hundred dollars on it, and that was a lot of money for that time.

Elder Dickerson was good to Lib and the rest of the children that were still at home. They loved him, because he was kind and generous to them as well as to Mama. But he had grown children from a previous marriage, lazy and dependent on their father. His oldest daughter, Henrietta, had separated from her husband and left her children with him. She had stayed in the home house with her mother and father until her mother died. Then Henrietta took over that little house in Eufala, and her father moved out to the farm.

Elder Dickerson's sons were going to help him farm his land, but they were too lazy to do anything. His oldest son, R.C., was supposed to do the plowing, but he was as sorry as all get out. He was a full-grown man with children, whose wife had kicked him out. Mama had to cook for him, and Lib couldn't stand him, because she said he always complained and wouldn't half work, though he made the children work hard. They would have to cut wood and carry it to the daughter in town, as well as vegetables, and even blackberries. She demanded so much without giving anything. Mama and her children had a hard time there. There was Lib and J.D. and Catherine and Frank T. In the meantime, my brother James had gotten a good break and was off at school in Nashville, Tennessee.

Reverend Dickerson only lived four years after marrying my mama, and when he died, Mama couldn't pay off the mortgage on his place. Even if she had been able to, those children by his first marriage would have gotten it. Mama didn't try to get anything from him at all. She said to his children, "Now you all can pay the mortgage off." But they wouldn't work, so the property went back into the hands of the receivers. I think about that now and realize that if I had been matured, I would have redeemed that farm. I learned later that after you have it and pay the taxes on it for so many years, it becomes yours. But I didn't know that at the time. It was beautiful land, and now some of the lots on that land are selling for a thousand dollars each.

While Mama was marrying Elder Dickerson in Eufala, I was over in Clio starting out on my own. That's where I met Jim Hayes. Jim's name was really Ernest, but they called him Jim for a nickname. Oh, boy, all the girls were after him, because he was a handsome, proud guy. Tall, tan, and terrific, we used to say. He knew it. He was stuck on himself. Nobody liked him, even the white men. He'd strut down that one street of Clio, with his head to the side. The ladies would kind of look around at him, and the men didn't like it. I didn't like him at first, myself. He kept on talking after me. He had one girl who thought she had him tied up, and just for spite, I was going to let her know that I could get him. That was the worst thing; I think that's why I got punished. He punished me but good.

By that time, I was rooming with a family named McCloud, a

bright-skinned lady. Jim would come calling, and we'd sit out there on the porch and talk. I was flattered, because he was the handsomest man in town and dressed better than anybody else around there. All the girls were hollering about him. So, I fell in love with him, I thought, and he went home with me and asked Mama for me. Mama said, "She's too young. She doesn't know you well enough." All that kind of thing. When we were by ourselves, Mama said to me, "He is not for you."

But I told Mama, "I love him, and I'm determined to marry him, whether you like it or not."

She said, "But you all weren't raised alike. You were raised in a religious home, and Jim wasn't." Mama had lived in Clio, and she still knew some of the old people there. I guess she had found out from them about his family. He never saw his daddy, because his daddy died before he was born. His mama raised him, and she was a sweet old lady. But he was raised around folks cussing and drinking and gambling. I wasn't used to any profanity or liquor in my family. He did all that stuff, but I didn't know it.

I went on and married him at the courthouse, in 1927, in the summer after school was out. I was eighteen years old. When I had told Mama I was determined to marry him, she said, "It's your bed; lie on it." I lay on it, too. I had such a time.

We went to live on a farm outside of Clio, in a little rented house. That little old house was a shotgun house. You walked on a little porch, and as you walked in the door on the right, there was another little door with a little room sitting on half of the porch. That was the extra bedroom. Then you walked into the big bedroom and then into the kitchen, and that's all there was. On that farm, there were just these shotgun houses. When you came in the back door into the kitchen, there was a shelf where you kept your water bucket. If you had a well, that was in the front yard. If you had to go to the spring, you had to go down under the hill somewhere to get water, but we did have a well. The kitchen just had a table and two chairs, and a cookstove and a few boxes.

I would scour the floor of that little house with boiling water once a week, on Saturday, so you could eat off it. Clean! You would use a corn-shuck mop and boiling water and potash soap. Then you would rinse off the floor with cold water and sweep it. You'd take your table and chairs out in the yard and scrub them with potash soap, sand, and boiling water. Then you'd rinse them. You'd take your mattresses, which were made of cotton and straw, out in the yard in the sun, stir up the insides and fluff them up and let them air. Then when you got in bed after your bath on Saturday night, you just died. Everything smelled so clean and fresh!

My mama came to visit me, my sister Beatrice came to see me, and they didn't want to believe it. I had been the tomboy. But I had every-thing whitewashed and cleaned and had even made a chocolate cake and wasn't even expecting company. My bed was made up, big old fat bed, clean, starched and ironed pillow slips sitting there on the top. The little shutter windows with white curtains that I had made, starched and ironed, flying out the windows. And I had canned some stuff, put up some preserves and vegetables like peas, and had them set up like ornaments on a shelf in the kitchen. They didn't want to believe it. Beatrice arrived one day with her husband and children, and there I was, in that immaculate house, cooking. Beatrice said, "I know I've come to the wrong house!"

I really tried; I didn't let people know what I was going through, married to him. Nobody knew but me, him, and God. I didn't have a hard time and run out and talk about it. I stayed there and took it. I was teaching, but he was messing up my money. I was putting it in the bank. He was farming, and we didn't have to borrow anything on the crop the way most farmers did, because I subsidized our farming with the little money I could put in the bank from my teaching. But we had a joint bank account; that was my husband, and we were supposed to be as one. He was getting money out for his gals and all his playing around. People told me about it, even the banker, who told me, "You haven't got a bit of sense." I said, "Don't talk to me like that about my husband." But they were just trying to warn me.

I would get tired, didn't even feel like making up the bed. I went to the doctor, who gave me a bottle about an inch in depth, full of a red medicine that I had to take by drops. When I took that bottle of medicine, it looked like I got energy from nowhere. Soon after that I found out I was pregnant. All along I had been praying to be able to have a baby who would look like his daddy, because he was such a handsome man, but to be industrious like I was. Here I was, telling God what to do.

When I got pregnant the doctor said the baby would come in June. On the twenty-second of April, my water broke, but I didn't know that had to happen. Nobody had told me that the water comes first. Jim wasn't around, and so I went to my mother-in-law's, about two blocks up the road. I told her what was happening and that I didn't understand. Poor silly soul, she should have known what it was, but she didn't. She said, "Well, bless the Lamb, daughter, come on up here and spend the night." On the way back home the next day, I had a terrible pain, and I thought I was constipated. I went over in the bushes, but nothing came. It would have been terrible if the baby had come then. But I didn't know I was fixing to have a baby. I went on home, and then I started hollering. My mother-in-law heard me and came to find out what was wrong. This was dry labor I was going through. She and my sister-in-law Cootney came along and got the doctor. He said the baby was coming. By that time Jim had come home, and he was peeping in the shutter window.

After the doctor told me I was going to have the baby, I said, "What? I can't have this baby! It's going to die, because it's not nine months!"

The doctor said, "My son is a seven-month baby. You have seven months in. It could live." That wasn't much consolation, because I was hurting. I had never known it was going to hurt that bad, and I was just screaming. The doctor said, "You don't need me. Just send for Angeline." She was the same midwife who had delivered me, and they sent for her and the doctor left.

I saw Jim looking in the window, and I said, "Get him out of here! Get him away!! He's the cause of all this!" Cootney jumped up there on the bed with me, to help. She weighed three hundred pounds, and here she was, trying to push me. I was kicking and hollering and screaming and going on. After awhile I had a BM, a hard one, and I picked that up and threw it against the wall. Nobody ever found it; I must have thrown it out the window. In that room there was just the bed, and a little table by the bed, and another table with quilts and things on it and a sheet over it, a chair and a box. And there was the mantelpiece with a few little things on it. But there wasn't anything for it to fall behind. Then the baby came, and they said, "Here the baby is!" But he wasn't crying. I had heard that you were supposed to slap their behind if they didn't cry, so there I was, telling the midwife what to do. I said, "Blow your breath in his mouth three times! Is there a cord around his neck?"

That old midwife said, "I know what to do." After a while, he started crying. So they washed him up and fixed him up, and here came old Jim in there, grinning. I said, "If this is what it costs to have a baby, this is it. I'm not going through all that pain again for any baby." But I nursed the baby and he got along fine. James David was born the twenty-third of April, 1928.

When things got so bad that I couldn't take it, I'd quit my husband and go home, but I never told Mama I was quitting him. She knew it, though. Sometimes when I would get home, I didn't have the money to go back to Clio. The fare was about a dollar and something. Mama would know; she'd say, "Sarah, when you get ready to go home, look in the Bible there and get a dollar." She knew I didn't have anything. When I had money and went home to Mama, I'd see if they needed groceries or anything like that, and I'd go get them. If I wasn't getting any groceries, she knew I didn't have any money to buy anything with.

Mama was a very conservative person. Sometimes she only made two dollars a week, or two dollars and a quarter, and a quarter was saved. When the need came, we had something. When she got down to the end of that budget of hers, she wasn't going to go get that saving money and use it for anything. That had to do for emergencies. She just stretched her budget to fit, and when it ran out, that was it. This was after I had gotten grown up some, and she was the head of the house; that's the way she managed it.

Jim was running around with women, throwing the money away, and jumping on me too, beating me up because I complained about his staying out all night over the weekends. Every weekend he would be out all night, but he'd always get back home in time to be in the field Monday. Where in this world could he be, staying out with the boys? I believed what he said, until one time when I was sympathizing with my sister-in-law and his aunt when they were complaining about their husbands, who were running-around men. I told them I felt sorry for them. My sister-in-law was tired of me saying that and told me, "You better feel sorry for yourself. Jim's got him one, too."

That kind of knocked the air out of my tires. I said, "I know that can't be true, because he told me he didn't love anybody or want anybody but me, and I believe it." The girl she said he was liking was fat, and he said he didn't like fat ladies, and he didn't like ladies to wear makeup, and she wore a lot of it. I thought they were just telling a story, and I decided to ask him.

In this little town of Clio, on Saturday evening the blacks would go to town. People from the farms would come in. There were benches all up and down the side of the street, and they'd sit there and eat ice cream and visit with one another. The young people would walk up and down the street courting. If there was a circus or show in town, they would go to those things.

I was in town with my sister-in-law, and Jim was in town too, but I didn't know where he was. I was going on home with them when they went home. Here came Sis, the one he was going with. Cootney, my sister-in-law, said, "Here she comes."

I said, "Here who comes?"

She said, "The woman Jim is going with."

I said, "Not that woman. She's got her face painted like a monkey, and fat, wearing a dress with a low waist and pulled right across her buttocks, and a short skirt." She had *wi-i-ide* hips, and her back part was going up and down like anything. I didn't want to believe it, and I said, "This can't be so."

In a little while Jim came along. In the meantime, my sister-in-law had gone home. I didn't go with them because I had decided I was going to find Jim and find out about this lie they told. He said, "Where's Cootney and Aunt Daisy?"

I said, "They've gone on home."

He said, "You didn't go with them?"

I said, "No, I was waiting to see you."

He said, "What you want to see me for?"

I said, "See you? How many Sis's do you know?"

He dropped his guard right there. He said, "Somebody's been talking to you, Sarah." If he had said, "What are you talking about?" I probably would have thought he was innocent. I knew then that he was guilty. He told me, "Don't you believe anything you hear people say until you see it. You go on home now."

I said, "No I'm not."

He said, "Yes you are."

I said, "I'm not going through the woods by myself." It was about a mile and a half.

He said, "I'll carry you." So he carried me home and then went out and stayed all night that night.

When he came in, he knocked on the door because I had all the latches on. I got up and opened the front door and opened the back door and slammed it like I was letting somebody out. He came in the front door, and I went there. The cotton field was right at the edge of our backyard, and the cotton was budding and was real high. He came through that house as fast as he could, running through that back to see who had gone out that door. I did that deliberately. There wasn't anybody in there, but I was trying to let him know that while he was off somewhere else, somebody could have been in his house. Then he jumped on me for nothing.

We had some wood behind the stove in the kitchen for cooking. It was heavy and seasoned. He struck me. I reached over there and got a piece of that wood and hit him, with all the might and main I could give him. He fell, and it frightened me, because I thought I had killed him. But I grabbed up another piece and stood over him, just in case. I said, "You hit me again, and I'll kill you. Hitting me for nothing, and you out running around all night long."

That stopped the hitting, but after that I just started turning from him. Jim had gotten a job putting up telegraph poles all across the fields, he and his brother and his cousin and a lot of men around there, the farmers whose crops were already in. He was gone five weeks before he came home. I had the baby, James David, by then. We must have been married about a year or two. While Jim was away, working on those telephone poles, I went to town one morning to get a water bucket and some other little things, and as I was walking down the street, I met his cousin Buck. I said, "Buck, when did you come?"

He said, "Well, we got in yesterday."

I said, "But has Jim come? I haven't seen him."

He said, "Yeah, Jim hasn't been home yet?"

I said, "No, where could he be?"

In a small place like Clio, all the whites knew each other, and all the blacks knew each other, and there wasn't anybody else in between, so I couldn't figure out what in the world he was doing. He made like he was so crazy about the baby. He loved steak, and I thought to myself, "I'll get him some steak." I got him a can of peaches, and I had some vegetables done. I thought I'd fix him a big old steak and some rice and run the gravy in it, because he liked that. So I got the steak and went on down the street on the way home, and ran into Buck again. Buck said, "You haven't seen him yet?"

I said no, and he laughed and said, "I'll tell you where he is, but don't tell him I told you."

I said, "Well, where is he?"

He said, "Down at Sis's house." She stayed down in what they called the Red Bottom. I went down there in the Bottom. In those days people didn't lock doors. I walked in the house, and there he was, sitting up there eating his dinner. She stayed in one room and had all her kitchen things in there at one end. He had on his BVDs and his pants on, but the suspenders were hanging down. He was in his sock feet, sitting up there eating steak she had bought.

I walked to that table and said, "Uh huh, you've been telling me to go by what I see and not by what I hear. Well I have *seen it*." I grabbed that steak off that table and threw it against the wall, both the plate, steak, and everything, and just started grabbing stuff and throwing it.

Then Sis came up there and grabbed me, and Jim jumped up and said, "Boy, don't you touch my wife!" Then I threw something at his head. All the cursing I have ever heard anybody say, I screamed it out as hard as I could, and if I had had a gun, I would have killed both of them. I was so angry, so frustrated, so *hurt*! Here this man is, couldn't come home to give his wife and his baby the first fruits of his love. That meant she was ahead of me, and I was his wife. That same fat Sister, and he said he didn't like fat folks and a lot of paint.

I left hotter than that stove and ran all up to the top of the hill. I still had my bucket. Some white man drove one of those cab things around the corner, and he got me in the car and carried me home. I was getting James David at his grandmama's and putting on his clothes; I was going to my mama's for good. She was saying, "Daughter, don't leave, you can stay here with me."

I said, "Why should I stay with you? That's your son. I don't want anything else to do with him; it makes me sick at the stomach to even think about it." After awhile, here he comes. I had that white cab man sitting out there waiting for me. Jim came up and told him to leave or he was going to blow his head off.

He said, "That's my wife, and I'll keep her." The man got scared and left. I stayed that night because I couldn't get to the train in time for the one train leaving out of there going to Eufala.

My mother-in-law got out of her bed and said, "I'll sleep on the pallet, and you stay in the bed."

During the night, I couldn't sleep, and I heard her telling Jim, "You can go and get in the bed with them."

He came in there, and I said, "No you don't. I heard what your mother said. She is supposed to be protecting me from you, and she's sending you to me." The next day I caught the train and went home, but I didn't stay then; I came back. This was one of the last times, when I made up my mind.

I had to go to summer school that summer, I think it was 1931, to keep up my certificate. I told him I had to go, and he said, "I won't have anybody to help me with the crop."

I said, "I've got to go to summer school to be able to teach. You get Sis to stay with you and help you while I'm gone. Since you're taking care of her anyway, I'll make it convenient so she'll be right here handy."

I told his mother that. She stayed right up the street. She said, "Lord, Darling"—her pet word was "bless the Lamb"—"bless the Lamb, you're going to do that?"

I told her, "Yes, bless the Lamb. It doesn't make any difference. I'm going to make it handy, where he can be with her and won't have to waste around messing around and lose his crop. I'll put it where he can get it." I meant that thing.

I went to Sis too and told her, "I want you to take care of my husband for me while I'm gone." And I meant it. It didn't make me a bit of difference; I could have seen them. My mother-in-law said, "Well, she isn't going to stay in that house."

But I said, "Why not? She can come out there and help in the field if she wants."

I went to summer school in Montgomery, at our state school— Alabama State Teachers' College. It didn't cost much, and I always saved that part of my money. Jim didn't get that. I got through summer school for six weeks. I was staying with an old teacher friend of mine, whose husband was a minister. She had two sons, and those two boys kept that house clean. They went to school at Alabama State too, smartest boys and good cooks. In the summertime, their mama took in washing and ironing, and they kept it up when she was out teaching school. I didn't have to pay much for room and board.

I didn't write a letter or a note to Jim, but that guy came up there. I came home from school one evening and the lady said, "Your husband is here." Jim came up there, and I told him I thought I had done right because I assumed he was getting along all right. He wanted to stay all night, and I told him I wasn't feeling so good. So he turned around and went on back.

When I got back home, my house was as clean as a whistle. She had done some canning, and my sister-in-law said, "Are you going to eat it?" I said, "Yep." One day I woke up in the morning and said, "I am through. It's just too bad, but I don't have any respect." James David was about two years old by then.

I had gotten so I would just as soon for a polecat with his musk on to lick me in my mouth as for Jim to even put his fingers on me. I just couldn't stand him. It wasn't hate, just disgust. I said, "Now, this is wrong, for a woman to have a husband and feel this way about him. I'm young." I was only about twenty-two then. I said, "There may be a time that I'll see somebody that I could love, but I'm hung up here with him."

I told him that was it. He said he was going to take my life. I said, "If that's God's will, let it be done." And I left. At school, when the children would see him coming, they'd say, "Miss Sarah, here comes Mr. Jim." They were afraid, but I said, "Let him come." Everybody was afraid of him; it was like who's afraid of the big bad wolf. Well, I wasn't. I didn't mind if he had taken my life. I didn't feel like he was going to take it. I didn't tell Mama anything about this stuff. But when I told him it was final, he went and got Mama up out of the bed and brought her. She had the flu. When she came down there, I said, "Mama, you didn't want me to marry him, and I did, because I was determined. I'm just as determined not to stay with him as I was to marry him."

She said, "Take me home; she means it." When I saw her and told her what I had been going through, she said, "My God, how did you stand it?"

I said, "Well, I wasn't going to tell you about it, because I was staying with him. I don't believe in staying with a man and talking about him. If you're going to stay there, stay there and shut up and take it, or leave if you have to and then talk about it, but don't do it while you're there." He went around and cried and begged and tried to get people to talk to me. He couldn't understand why I was quitting him, because he had stopped hitting me and being mean to me a long time earlier. I told him, "All the things you have done to me have turned me against you, and I don't feel that I could treat you right as a wife."

When I divorced him, he didn't care anything about that woman. He got another one and married her, and did the same thing to her. They separated and then he married again. But before he died up in Akron, Ohio, his brother said he said, "I never had but one wife, and that was

Sarah." He came one time after Rice and I got married, and I invited him in and introduced him to Rice. He told Rice, "You sure got a good wife." That's all he said. He had everything he could want: a good wife, good health and strength, and he was a good farmer, but I don't know, it wasn't enough for him.

CHAPTER FIVE

Hard Times and Florida Debut
(1929–1933)

When I decided to leave Jim Hayes, I decided there would be no more husbands for me. As long as I lived, there wouldn't be another man. I felt like all men were the same. That's bad, but that's what I thought. When James David was about two years old, I went back home during the summer, to stay.

I had gone back home on one of my visits before I quit James Hayes for good. I said to Mama, "I'm surprised at you, marrying Elder Dickerson. He and Papa were good friends."

She looked at me just as calmly, and she said, "If you had stayed home to help me with these other children, I wouldn't have married him. I needed some help, and he has been very kind and good to all of us." Praise the Lord, I had to get help from him too, before it was done with. I had to carry my son there, when I left Jim, because I got a job in a school near Eufala, and I had to leave James David with Mama.

That school was called Rocky Mount, not too far from Eufala. If I had had transportation, I would have come home every night, but I didn't have it, and so I would just come home on weekends. It was a Rosenwald school, about fifteen or twenty miles outside of Eufala. Professor Rosenwald allocated money—one of the Rosenwalds was a millionaire—for schools in communities where there wasn't any school. It was a kind of grant that came through the county.

This school was a very nice one, and the principal was from Atlanta, Mr. Whaley. I stayed with these people called Forbes. They were big farmers out in that area. People used to think that teachers had expertise on everything. They thought you knew everything and they could go ask the teacher. I didn't know nearly as much as they did, but they thought it, so you had to pretend you knew about some things. I had a good time teaching there. The principal was lazy. He wasn't a good math person, so I had to teach all the math. He wasn't good in geography; I taught all the geography. I had the first three grades, and he had the last three, but I had to do arithmetic and geography for all of them. He didn't know how to do his register. Now he had finished college, and I hadn't. I had finished high school by going to summer school and had had one year on my college credits. Here he was a graduate of a school in Atlanta. It wasn't Clark, and it wasn't Spelman. It was Morehouse or Atlanta University. But he couldn't even add, and I had to fix his register as well as mine.

He told me about his girlfriend in Atlanta and said they were going to get married. I said to myself, and this is the bad part of it, I'm going to see how desirable I am. Jim had about knocked all the juice out of me. I had said I'd never marry anymore, but I wanted to be desired. So I flirted around with him a little bit. That was all there was to it. He was getting ready to go back to Atlanta for the Thanksgiving holiday. I'd go home every weekend, because it was so close. I pretended that I was sad that he was going away, that he was going to get married, and I was going to be left. Testing, testing, testing. I got so mad at myself, and Lib wanted to kill me. He said, "Who's talking about going to Atlanta, honey? I'm going to come and spend Thanksgiving with you."

Oh, my gosh, I didn't want that guy at our house, and I didn't know what Mama was going to think about some man coming and spending time at my home. Back then, that was practically asking a girl to marry him, or worse than that, you must be sleeping with him and not married. I didn't know how in the world I was going to work that out. So I made like I had dreamed about it, and said, "You go ahead to Atlanta; she is going to be disappointed." I said every kind of lie I could think of to get out of that mess.

I had started walking up home with him, and Lib started crying and running, because she figured that here was more work and somebody else to feed when there was hardly enough for the family to eat. She said, "I don't want to be waiting on that old Scratch, old Yankee man coming in here and me having to do more work." He was only from Atlanta, but Lib just didn't like to be bothered with him. She and Catherine were mad, but Mama tried to be nice.

Mama said, "Well, after all, he's our guest." But he went down there and cut up wood like I don't know what. He fell right into it.

I had to clean up the house when I got there, because it was in a mess. I said to Lib, "Well, I hated for him to come and catch the household messed up, but I wasn't here and y'all weren't keeping it straight, and Mama was working all the time."

Lib said, "I bet he came from a dump. No wonder he's so mad about you." Lib just about had a stroke at ten years old, because he stayed for the whole weekend and would sit there at meals just consuming everything on the table.

I had to get rid of him, because I wasn't thinking about marrying him or anybody else. Then I started gradually pulling myself back where I wanted to be, and being myself instead of pretending to be in love with him and afraid I was going to lose him.

I had been just trying it out, to see how much power I had, but it's dangerous doing something like that. I would flirt a little bit, but only up to a point, because some of those things you have to pay off, the kind of price I wasn't going to pay. I really had my morals up straight.

Whenever I went home to Mama's for the weekend, I always brought something for the other children. I'd make the Easter dresses for Lib and Catherine and send those every year. If I had any money when I got home, I'd check and see what was in the kitchen, and then I'd get my brother J.D. and tell him, "Get the wagon, and let's go to town." I'd buy them some groceries and fill the larder. When I came home, I always cooked up good things for them, and so they knew they were going to have a good time when I came home. But one thing about it, I made them clean up too. Lib would say, "I was cleaning up the hardest I could, and here you come, fussing at me."

I stayed at Rocky Mount for about two years, and then I got a school in Clayton, Alabama, at the county seat of Barbour County. I would get James David and carry him down there to spend the weekends with me, but he was still staying with Mama. He stayed with Mama off and on like that until I got married the second time and moved to Jacksonville. When I got to Clayton, they had four teachers, including me. This was before I went down to Panama City. The principal was named Mealy, ugliest man I have ever seen in my life, but immaculate. His shirts were just as neat, collars just right, his clothes, his shoes, his cleanliness. He was just perfect, very intelligent, but ugly as homemade sin. But he had a growing thing about him. The more you knew him, the less ugly he was.

Two of the women were already married, and one was single but very homely. He wasn't about to be bothering with any of them. One day we had something going on at the school, some kind of program that night. To get to where I was rooming, you would have to go over a fence with a stile. We left the school; he walked home with me across the stile. I inadvertently fell into his arms, getting over that fence, to see what it felt like. Felt real nice. Then I pulled back and went on to my place. Then he started trailing me for good. Boy, I really ducked him every time I could. One night I just broke down and cried and told him I was afraid. I said, "I've had such a hard time with my husband. I feel you're too nice a person to get yourself confused with me. I'm not sure what I want to do or where I want to go." He left me alone after a while.

I was just kind of trying my luck around different things, but I had really planned never to marry again. I thought the only good thing a man could do for me was to give me a job, and tell me "Good Morning" or "Good Evening." That's all I needed from them, and I meant that thing too. But it wasn't really like that. I was still human, and I was still young, and I still had sexual desires like any other normal human woman. I tried to fool myself with thinking I didn't need any man. For seventeen years between my second and third husbands, that went on. I almost forgot that I was on any gender side. The longer you go, the stronger you get, and the less sex you think about. That goes for churchgoing, eating, smoking, drinking, dope—anything can be habitual. The more you do it, the more you want to. If you can once stop, you can just keep on. I just went on about my business.

While I was teaching in Clayton, I got very sick. We had had a program at the school that night, and I was hurrying to get ready to go back for it. I did my own cooking, so I wanted some white potatoes, fried with some white bacon. I'd fry the bacon first and then the potatoes. I must not have gotten them all the way done, being in a rush to get to school, and I ate them. That night around ten or eleven o'clock, I had acute indigestion and was as sick as I had ever been in my life. I felt like I was dying, and they took me over to Eufala to the hospital. That was the best hospital in the area.

Not thinking anything about it, they didn't even let my mama know. But Mama found out, and she came and brought James David. Lib and J.D. and Baby were sitting around the fire praying for me to be alive. I guess we all are superstitious some way. There's an old saying in our family that if you see a spider hanging from the wall, and he falls, somebody in the family will be sick or die. There was a spider hanging there as they all sat, looking in the fire. Here came this spider, just swinging. J.D. jumped up and grabbed the spider and busted him open before he fell, and J.D. said, "Now Sarah's going to be all right."

When the doctor in the hospital got me to relieve myself of that food, I was all right. The doctor said I hadn't digested it. I guess I had eaten hurriedly in order to get to school.

After I taught in Clayton, I had a school in Ariton, which was not far from Clio, and there I ran into a family named Dixon. There was a man named Dixon who was renting a four-horse farm, and he was a good farmer, really knew how to farm. A four-horse farm is 160 acres. He raised plenty of cotton, corn, hogs, children. He had it all to himself. He had married a woman with two girls. The woman he married had children for him, and her two daughters had children for him. He didn't allow any man on his premises, unless it was the man he was renting the land from. Even that man stood out in the yard and talked to Mr. Dixon, but he didn't bother him because he was a good farmer. He had a Model T Ford.

All those children would come to school to me. They came up there and told me, when I was trying to write down the family's names for my records and so I could contact the family. When they told me they were first cousins and sisters and brothers, aunts and uncles all at the same time, I said, "Well, no, I'm afraid you all have me confused."

"No'm, we're first cousins and sisters and brothers."

I decided I wouldn't argue the point. I just wrote the names down. When I got back home, I told my landlady. She said, "They're not lying." And she went on to tell me about the man's problem. There I was. I had never seen anything like that or heard of it.

The wife seemed to accept it until she got tired, and one day she ran away from him and went to a nearby town, maybe twenty-five or thirty miles. He heard where she was, so he got in his T-model Ford. It had been raining hard, and he went to hunt for his wife. While he was going, he went up this slippery red clay road and had a wreck and turned the car over and killed himself. That man was a smart man in a way; he had all kinds of insurance. Lots of black folks didn't have any insurance, so that when they died, their family would have to get together and get a box or make one, and bury the person themselves.

When the wife found out he was dead, she came back, and they buried him. Then she and those girls had themselves a ball! The men flocked over there like buzzards behind carrion, and those women gave them anything they wanted. "You want a pig?" Oink, oink, there went a pig. They were so glad to have other men's company. And they were ordering from the catalog company named National Bellas Hess, and from Sears Roebuck. They ordered dresses and all kinds of things. After about eight months they were down to practically no money, but they still had plenty of food on the farm. I don't know what finally happened to them, but that Mr. Dixon really left a family. The wife had two children before she married him, and then she had about four for him. The daughters had about five apiece. There were something like fourteen children, and they all worked on the farm.

Then I moved to a place called Pinkard, Alabama, in Dale County, where I had a lovely school. In the community, people were so nice and respectful that I really had a good time there. The landlady had a little grandchild who was a spoiled brat, but we got along just fine anyway.

I was always thinking of ways out, how I could get the job done.

Some of the parents would grumble and fuss all the time. Once a friend of mine told me, "Sarah, never have anything to do with the men in the community where you teach. The fact is, none of them are fit for a teacher anyway. I wouldn't lower my dignity." Then I came to find out that she was beating the poor farmers out of their hams, bales of cotton, hogs. They would get their crops in and give that teacher the money. A man would go to town to sell a bale of cotton, and she'd get half of the money. When she would get ready to go home to Montgomery, her car would be loaded with hams, sides of meat and things that those men would give her. I said to myself that she must have thought I would give her some trouble. I wondered when we went to summer school how she was able to have so much money and have such pretty clothes, when we were making the same salary. Well, some of those wives in the community found out that she was getting things from their husbands, and they got rid of her. Teachers can do most anything they want to now, but in my day, what they deemed your character determined your job. If the school board disapproved of you, they would let you go in a minute. You didn't have anybody to defend you.

One time a friend named Laura Will Floyd and I went from Pinkard to Ozark, the county seat, to get our money. My landlord's son-in-law, whose name was Gus, had an old A-model Ford, and I asked him to loan it to me. I didn't have any driver's license, but I could keep a car in the road. He loaned me his car, and I went and picked up my friend Laura, who had a school about five miles from me, and we drove to Ozark. The courthouse stood in the middle of the square. At one time there was a big watering trough, but cars parked there after people stopped using horses. I parked the car, and we went out and got our paychecks. I didn't know how to back out, so I walked around until a man came up in a car and I asked if he would back the car out for me and head it in the right direction.

When we got back, Gus, the man who had lent me the car, was worried to death. He thought I was just going to my friend's house, and when I didn't come back, he got someone to take him there. They told him, "They've gone to Ozark." He thought I was going to kill myself, but there weren't many cars on the road then, and I drove that thing back, put my friend out, and returned the car. Gus said, "Miss, I can't let you have my car anymore. I didn't know you were going to town."

One day that man went to town to tend to some business. He had just left to go to town, when his car came back. The landlady said, "I wonder who's driving Gus's car." I didn't pay any attention, because I thought it was one of his men friends. He and his wife were separated, and he stayed at the house right next door to me. The man jumped out, and Gus was in the car, dead. A white man who was mentally deranged saw Gus coming up and said, "Here comes a nightbird," and just raised his rifle and shot. That white man's parents were all upset about it, but it was too late. That was a scary thing to me; he had asked the landlady, "See if the teacher wants me to bring her something back from town." I had said no, thank you, that I didn't need anything. And that man got killed.

I have seen a lot of hard things. I had a friend named Martha Jackson, whose father was one of the trustees and stewards of one of the churches my daddy pastored outside of Eufala. He was a great farmer who had about four or five hundred acres of land. We used to call people like that Big Dogs. He was the first black man to have a car, and all of the things that people wanted. His name was Tobe Jackson. Martha was his baby girl and was very tall—six feet or more—and a pretty person. We must have looked funny together, because I was very short. She was our county supervisor.

Before she became supervisor, there had been a family tradition between the Jacksons and the Cunninghams, a feud like the one between the Hatfields and the McCoys. It started way back in the granddaddys' days and continued up into the time when I was a child and Papa was still alive. A Cunningham boy loved one of Martha's sisters, and she loved him. She wanted to get married, but her daddy said, "No, you will never marry a Cunningham." The girl got pregnant by the Cunningham boy, and then Tobe said, "You're going to marry her so the baby will have a respectable name, but you are not going to stay with her. I won't have you hanging around." The boy married her; he wanted to marry her anyway. When the baby came, he wanted to see his baby, but Tobe said no. The boy took it to court and won the right to see the baby.

There were two churches, a Baptist and a Methodist church. A preacher would only come once a month to each church, so on the Sundays when there was no preacher, there would only be Sunday school. All the folks who loved to go to church would go to the one that had the preacher when he came. One Sunday, they were all at the Baptist church when Tobe Jackson, a Methodist, came up with his grown boys and his daughter who had the baby. He told her, "I want you to stay in the car, and if you see your husband, call him to the car." She did, and the daddy and the brothers came out of there shooting. Out on the church ground the Cunninghams killed one of her brothers. The Jacksons were after the Cunninghams, but the Cunninghams had guns too. They killed a bystander and the Cunningham boy who was her husband. The Cunninghams had a big plantation too, and they got lawyers from Montgomery to come down and fight their case. When they ended up, they didn't have a pot to pee in, either family. The lawyers had milked them clean. That poor girl lost her mind, and Jackson died, almost a pauper. All of that because of a family feud. Every time my friend Martha would talk about that, she would burst out crying. She would talk about how devastating family feuds are and how many people they can hurt. Papa would go talk to both families and try to get them to stop fighting. He would say, "Your children are dead, and you can't bring them back. Pray and ask God to forgive you, and take that hate out of your hearts."

By 1930 or 1931, Elder Dickerson had died, and Mama had moved back to her farm, but we really didn't have anything. In 1933, I went back to Rocky Mount to teach again, close to Mama. That was the time when I got the shoes for J.D. I had a little change and bought them some things that were needed. School started, but there was still no money in the family, and my brother J.D. didn't have any shoes. He was a big old boy about seventeen years old. We ran out of food again, and Mama couldn't find anything, and I couldn't either. I took J.D. and said, "Come on, let's get you some shoes."

He said, "Where are you going?"

I said, "We're going to get some food. Hitch up the horse." I had decided to myself that day, whether I was going to prostitute or what, I was going to get it.

We got near town, and I had one of those old warrants with me from the school board. I went to Mr. Hap Gregory's grocery store. He said, "Sarah, I'm sorry, but I can't take any more of those warrants. I have them here, and I can't pay my bills if I keep taking those things in, because I don't know when they're going to be negotiable."

I said, "I understand." I went to another grocery store—same thing. Then I went to Mr. Jake Oppenheimer, who was a Jew and ran not a grocery store, but a dry-goods store. Mr. Oppenheimer knew every prominent Negro in town, and he knew of my family, Lizzie's children. Most all the white people knew Lizzie; Mama wasn't an aristocrat but she was prominent and recognized by everyone. So were her children. I went to him, and he knew me too.

I have never told such a slick lie in my life, and I didn't even think about it. When I went in there to him to ask for aid, I didn't tell him that I had been to the other people. I didn't tell him that I wanted him to take a warrant. I said, "Mr. Oppenheimer, I have some cows for sale in Clio, but I need some money until I can get those cows. I wondered if you would hold this warrant and let me have some money until I can get the cows sold."

He said, "Yes. How much do you need?"

Isn't that some kind of approach? I hadn't thought about that; I had thought I was going to go to him just like I had gone to the rest of them. I knew I couldn't get any groceries from him, but I just wanted him to lend me some money on this warrant so I could buy some food. That was my plan, but when I got in there, these other words came to me. I didn't have any cow anywhere to sell. Well, I took about twenty dollars, and I said, "By the way, do you have any shoes to fit my brother?"

He said, "Yeah, I've got a pair of shoes. Come here, boy." Carried him over there and got him a pair of brand-new shoes. I mean he was *barefooted*, and we were coming to the fall of the year and nowhere to get any shoes. My brother was so happy, and to this day he talks about how glad he was. I tell him how good he was to Mama, and he was. She called him her old man. But he tells me how good I was to him.

I took that money, and we didn't go back to the stores that had turned me down. They were the two best stores, but I went to another one. It was a good-enough store. Those other two should have helped me, because we had been trading with them, but since they didn't, I wasn't going to give my money to them. At the other store, we loaded up that wagon with *hard* groceries—meal, lard, white bacon (it was cheap then, about ten cents a pound), syrup. And I went on and got three or four loaves of light bread—that was something special for us— and some lemons and sugar so we could have some lemonade, and some ground-up beef so that we could make us some sandwiches. And I had *money* left over.

Mama just cried when we got back home. She said, "I knew you were going on to town, but I wasn't looking for you to find anything."

I said, "You know, you used to sing a song one time when you went down to the Woman's Ridge and got that half-dried corn and came back and we ground it up in the meat grinder and sifted it until we could make hoecakes. That was the best-tasting cornbread I ever ate in my life. You started singing that song, 'Jesus included me. When the Lord said, "Whosoever will," He included me.' So I'm his child too, and I don't have any business starving. I'm singing the same thing, 'Jesus included me too.'"

Mama said, "Bless your heart."

We went in, and we had a feast. J.D. talks about that now. He says, "I love my sister, who gave me shoes when I needed them." That same next week, he joined the C.C. Camp. That was kind of like a part of the army, the Civilian Conservation Corps, and thirty-five dollars a month is what they paid him. All of it he sent up, *all* of it to Mama. He said, "I get plenty to eat, and if there's anything I need, I'll get it from Mama."

Mama said, "Well, I'm only going to use a part, only what I need." Mama was a really conservative person and wasn't going to spend up anybody's money. She wasn't going to spend all that money, thirty-five dollars a month.

We started living better. The very next week, it came out in the paper that a series of those warrants were negotiable as of that date. Mine happened to be in that series, the one I had given him. It was worth thirty-five dollars, so Mr. Oppenheimer owed me fifteen dollars. I had two more warrants to cash after that. I was home free then, and in the meantime Mama was getting a little something from J.D., so we got over that hump.

It's like the hymnist: "Through many dangers, toils, and snares I have already come; T'was Grace that brought me safe thus far, and Grace will lead me home." I've been through a lot of things, and nobody knew about it but the inside of the family. Outside, folks never did talk, because we were still fine. No, thank you. We didn't go to any of our neighbors and ask them to lend us a dollar, to lend us some meal, even when we knew we had no bread in the house. But before night came, we could eat. People always thought that we had some money, but we didn't have anything but pride. Pride can take you a ways, and it can let you be hungry too. But we never turned down anything that anybody gave us. We always said thank you, whether we could use it right then or not. There always came a time when we could reach back and get that thing, and if we couldn't use it, there was somebody else that we could share it with.

The week after that Oppenheimer thing happened, I asked God for forgiveness for that lie I told. I never could understand, up until this day, how the Lord let me come up with that lie. There was a lie in it, because I didn't have any cows. The reason it bothered me was that I had been praying all along for a blessing, and yet when the blessing came, there was a lie in it. I couldn't understand how the Lord let it happen right away, before the week was out. I decided that there are some things the Bible says I'm not supposed to know, and I was going to stop worrying about it. It's kind of like the story, I stepped on a pin and the pin bent, and that's the way the story went.

In the meantime, I put James David in kindergarten, with a girl named Lucy Coats who was a friend of mine. She was an old maid who lived with her mother, but the children loved her, and she took a lot of time with them. So James got his ABCs and was able to write his name and do a little spelling and a little reading.

When he got to be six and went into the first grade, he started crying because of all of those strange children. That school was in Eufala and had all the grades all hooked up there together in one building. James David carried on and said, "I want Lib! I want Lib!" The principal didn't know her by that nickname, because in the school Lib was known as Elizabeth Webb. So the principal went around to every class-room and said, "Is there anybody around here named Lib?" Finally they found her, and she went to James and calmed him down. After that, he didn't have any problem. He did pretty well in school.

School was short in 1933, because the state's money gave out. I went to Columbus, Georgia, where I had an uncle. I thought if I could get some domestic work there, it would tide us over, because we had fallen back into a financial slump. This was during the bad times in the depression.

My uncle was so proud that his niece was a teacher that he wasn't about ready for her to go getting domestic work. That was a letdown for him; he had bragged to everybody that his sister's daughter the schoolteacher was coming there. I told him I didn't give a durn about that; I was hungry and needed food for my family and wanted an honest job. I couldn't get any work there, anyway, because he wouldn't let me out to go look for it. I didn't know where any employment agency was or how to go about doing that.

So I went back home, but I went by my cousin's who lived out in the country near Fort Mitchell. She fixed a lunch for me. Now, I was forty-six miles from home, but she knew that I'd need that lunch. That's how slow those buses were running back then. She fixed me a shoe box full of biscuits and fried chicken, and I caught the bus in Columbus. On this bus was one other person, a white lady from Atlanta, Georgia, named Mrs. Wells, a young, pretty woman. The bus driver made his money carrying mail, too. He drove what we would call a station wagon now, but back then we called it a bus. I took my lunch out, after I got down the road a piece, and the lady looked at it grudgingly. On the spur of the moment I said, "Won't you have some?"

She looked and said, "Looks mighty good. Did you cook it?"

I told her, "No ma'am, my cousin did."

She said, "How would you like to come work for me?"

I said, "I would like it. Where do you live?"

She said, "Panama City," and got my name and address and said, "If I send for you, will you come?"

She meant Panama City, Florida, but I thought she meant the Panama Canal. But I said, "Yes ma'am," because I had gone up to Columbus looking for work. The schools were closed back down at home, and I hadn't even gotten all my money from the time I had taught. I didn't have anything but those warrants, and no job and no money.

I got home from Columbus and told Mama I had met that lady and how nice she was. I said, "I can't go to Panama."

And Mama said, "Why can't you? You're not doing anything here." That very next week, I got a letter with a money order, not a ticket but a money order. I could have cashed it and not said a word to that lady. I went to Panama City and left James David with Mama. That was a blessing in disguise. It was my Florida debut.

I stayed on the premises with that lady. They were the nicest couple. He was a dentist, Dr. Wells. They stayed out in the suburb of the town, right on the bay, in a two-story wood house. The houses were far apart, with big lawns and palm trees and pretty flowers. The back of the Wells' house was the prettiest. The front of the house faced the ocean, but the back faced the street, and that's where the flowers and the lawn were. Most everybody who visited them went in the back door.

That bay looked just like the ocean; you could look way across it and not know whether the bay runs into the ocean or what. There was a beautiful beach along the bay, with clean white sand, going for miles. I would get up early in the morning and go down to the beach and see the sun come up over the water, and just walk in the sand up and down the beach and kind of hum. I wished the whole world was like that. It was so peaceful, looking across the water; it just looked like to me I was in another world. I would get up early in the morning and walk down and look at that water, and then I would go back up to my room and get myself ready and fix their breakfast.

Almost every morning I burned the toast and would have to scrape it. I didn't know the doctor paid any attention to it and didn't realize I had been scraping it. I thought I had them fooled. One day I made the toast nice and brown, didn't burn it. The doctor said, "Oh, no!"

I said, "What's the matter, Doctor?"

He said, "My toast hasn't been burned and scraped!"

Boy, I just hollered! I said, "Lord, I didn't think you knew I was burning that toast."

Mrs. Wells was a very creative person and liked to do things with her hands, kind of like my mama. She really taught me a lot. We painted the fireplace over, we made over clothes that her mother sent her. She gave me some pretty clothes and helped me to make them over for myself. I would go to the black church in the community there, and I just had myself a ball on Sunday. I'd fix their dinner, and I'd go up there with my folks and stay all the rest of the day, and some of them would come home with me at night.

The Wellses had a grape arbor right over the back entrance, with muscadine grapes growing all over the door to my little room. My room was out in the back, but it was hooked onto the rest of the house. When the grapes got ripe, I carried some of them into my room and made some grape wine. The Wellses would drink wine, but it was just like Riunite or something. I let them taste my wine one day, and they went wild over it. Dr. Wells said, "Well, now you're going to make me some wine."

I stayed with those people two years, and Mrs. Wells was just as nice to me as she could be. Then I went back to teaching, and they got me a school not far from Panama City, in a place called Westbay. That was almost like another world, on the most beautiful bay you have ever seen in your life. You could just get up early in the morning and see the sun coming up, like it was coming up from the ocean.

In Westbay I stayed in a house that you see on an old beach or at an old fishing camp. It had been painted, maybe years before, but the storms and the wind had washed it off, down to the wood. But it was a good stout house that had about five or six big, airy rooms. It took a lot of walking to get through it. The landlady that I stayed with was the cleanest woman that I ever saw in my life. That woman bathed twice a day. Her house wasn't loaded with furniture, but it was as clean as it could be, everywhere. Her husband worked at this fishing camp or whatever it was up the road, and she kept her house. She would get in that tin washtub and scrub herself all over.

They didn't have any children. He was kind of quiet and nice, and she was a pretty woman. He had a sister with a lot of children, who lived there in the community, and there were about three or four other families with children. That was all, but they wanted to get up a school for those twenty-five or thirty children. All those children were in one room for school. I would let the little ones stay by their big sisters or brothers so they could feel safe. But I had them all in sight, so I could see to them all getting their lessons. Sometimes the little ones would learn from the big ones. We didn't have any desks, just chairs. At one of those schools, one of the fathers made a kind of long table with two long boards. That helped out a lot.

That house where I stayed was right on the beach. You would just walk down some steps, and there you were. The landlady and her husband had a dog called Rock, and I could just walk up and down the beach with him, along the edge of the water. We would go down there every afternoon, crabbing when the tide came in. The dog would see a crab and bark, and we'd go after it. We would fill croker sacks with crabs and come back and have a crab boil. We'd clean the crabs and make crab gumbo and all kinds of good things to eat. And fish! Little whitings. We'd fish for them with strings.

That place must have been a fish camp a long time ago. There was a restaurant or something, where the people worked. A white lady owned the restaurant, and the colored people worked out there. They just had a one-teacher school. It was so quiet and nice that I enjoyed it I think more than any other school I had.

I taught there a year, and then I went back home to Alabama to visit. While I was at home with Mama, I got a letter from Mrs. Wells to come back to Panama City for another job that had opened up down there. She said I could stay with her. I went back down to Panama City and took the job they had found for me in a little old place, Bayou George, Florida, that was about ten miles from Panama City. That was a turpentine place, a flip for the flappers, and a rat race if there ever was one. The school had closed down, but they had decided to reopen it. They knew about my work at Westbay and thought I would be a good person to get the school started back up.

During the week, I would live in Bayou George and teach in the school, but every weekend, I would go into Panama City and stayed with a friend named Gussie, who had a room with Reverend and Mrs. Eddings. They were lovely people, but Mrs. Eddings is the one who told me I shouldn't have anything to do with the men in the town because they weren't good enough for me. Years later, when I was living in Jacksonville, I heard that the young man I had been interested in, who was a member of our church, was her boyfriend. Now she was about four years older than me. Maybe she had that in mind when I was rooming with her, but I don't think she was doing anything with that boy yet. Maybe she was just jealous of me and Gussie and just thought that we might get at the reverend.

Gussie was a wild one. Gussie liked drinking, but I didn't. I told her that I never drank. She had a boyfriend working at the bar, and he got off one night around about twelve and came by and brought Gussie some liquor. I was lying up there in the bed asleep, but she woke me up. Now I liked wine. She woke me up and told me to take this blackberry wine. I was half asleep, and I drank a big gulp of it. That stuff did burn, and it didn't taste like blackberry wine. It was sloe gin or Grand Dad or some kind of stuff. That next morning I woke up, and it was a good thing it was on a Saturday. I tried to walk, and I couldn't. I said, "I'm so thirsty." I went and got me a big, cold glass of water, and I got as sick as a dog. I had drunk all that whiskey. Gussie was just laughing. I said, "I'm going to kill you, and your boyfriend too. Y'all just wanted to make me drunk. What else happened?" I couldn't see why anybody wanted to get drunk and feel that bad afterward. It's not worth it.

You drove into Bayou George on a state highway from Panama City. On the left was the bayou—like a lake with a lot of fish in it. It was a beautiful place, but about a block after you passed the bayou, the houses started on the left. They were just little old smoky, smutty-looking, shacky wooden houses with tar-paper roofs and shutter windows. Some of the houses were a little bigger, maybe because some of the overseers had lived in them when they were first built. But by this time all the people living in them were black. Across the road from the houses was the railroad track, and the little church building was across the track.

On up further on the left side of the road was the commissary and a big house where the man who ran the commissary and his wife lived. The commissary was a barnlike structure, kind of a general store. Nobody had any cars around there, so they didn't sell gas. They had a beautiful garden. That was all there was to Bayou George. The mailman came out of Panama City. The train passed through there and grabbed the outgoing mail with something like a shepherd's crook. It wouldn't stop for passengers.

About two miles further down the road, you turned left, and there were two palaces down there. Some wealthy people from the North had *fine* houses, big two-story mansions. The people in one of those places stayed the year round and had a maid and a chauffeur. They had their own cottage. The chauffeur was the maid's son, whose name was Willie. Sometimes he would carry me into town. He was telling me about how he had fallen in love with me, but I wasn't studying about him. I told him he was too young. But I was glad to get that ride into town.

The people who owned the other house only came down in the summertime, and their maid stayed on to keep the house for them. She was a liquor-head. When the people came back down, she had got drunk and smoked up the house with the kerosene stove. She had put on the lady's gowns and lay up in the bed as drunk as Cooter Brown when they came in. They got rid of her, but they got her back because she was a good cook. I ate some of her food, and good God! That lady could cook, and I never tasted any better.

Here we are: a bunch of turpentine workers who go around and scrape the pine trees to get the sap. Their wives stayed home, because there wasn't anything for them to do unless they worked for the white family of the owner of the turpentine still. That lady had a big garden, a milk cow or two, and then she ran the commissary too. But most of those black wives wouldn't even plant a garden. They'd go to the creek and sit there and fish all day, talking and dipping snuff. They didn't catch much fish. On Saturday, they'd go to the commissary and get bacon and beans and rice and peas and syrup and coffee—stuff to eat during the week. On Sunday they'd have canned salmon, cooked up with onions and served on rice.

In Bayou George, I roomed with a lady named Mrs. Robinson, whose husband was a minister. The people in the community must have thought that the minister's wife would be a little better than the rest of them, and so it would be the right place for me to stay. She had just quit him before I went there to teach. He seemed to be a nice old man. That poor old man wasn't much of a preacher, just a jackleg preacher. In the town, there was only one church; actually it was just a house that the turpentine man had given them to have Sunday services in. One week the Methodist people would have worship; the next week the Baptist people would have worship; and the next week the Holiness folks would have their service. It was a three-in-one church. All of them went to church, more or less. There wasn't anywhere else to go.

I always liked peace, and I asked Mrs. Robinson why she had quarreled with her husband. It was over a small thing. She accused him of molesting their daughter, but she was a grown woman and married, and I didn't believe that old man would do such a thing. And she was mad at her sister and hadn't spoken to her in thirteen years. The sister lived about five miles from her. My landlady belonged to the Holiness church. They say they are sanctified and holy, without sin, because they are full of the Holy Ghost. And yet she hated her sister. I should have smelled a rat then, but I didn't.

Her house was one of these turpentine houses. They were little huts that were all alike. You walked in the house, and there was a big room to the right. To the left was another, smaller room, and then the kitchen right behind it. Three rooms. I was in the little room to the left. The landlady slept in the big room on the right. There wasn't a wooden door to my room, just a curtain, and it was torn up. I just took one of my sheets and split it, and hung it up there to make it look decent. They had newspaper and Sears Roebuck catalog paper all over the walls and the ceiling. You make up starch and use that to glue the paper to the wall. But in that house, the paper was hanging off the walls. I got up there on a chair in my room and pasted some of the paper back. I brought some more stuff from Panama City to make it look nicer. That woman said I was taking over her house.

She finally took her husband back, because she didn't have any money. That old man was a pitiful thing. I don't see how he even worked. He would get up early in the morning and try to fix his breakfast before going to work. Sometimes I'd get up and make biscuits for him. She lay in bed and just let me make his breakfast. There was no door you could close between their bedroom and the kitchen, just an open door frame. When I would come back after the weekend in Panama City, I would bring them something fresh, like some stew beef, because I knew they didn't have much. They would have their salmon on Sunday, but during the week they just had a little bacon and meal and syrup.

One of the neighbor ladies had told me, "Your landlady is saying you are about to take her husband." That was because I was making his breakfast.

I said, "Well, I'm going to find out."

When school was out one day and I was coming home, she caught me on the way. The school was in the church building. I said, "Mrs. Robinson, I'd like to talk to you for a minute."

She said, "All right."

I said, "I understand that you are saying I am bothering your husband by cooking for him and doing other little nice things for him. I thought I was helping you. I'm so sorry if you thought there was anything else."

She said, "Yeah, I did say that."

I said, "Well, that's a lie, and the truth is not in it. You told me that he wasn't any good sexually and that he doesn't have any money. What the hell do you think I want with him?"

I went to the sheriff. I knew him because he was a friend of Dr. and Mrs. Wells and would come there for dinner sometimes. I think he had tasted some of my wine too. He knew I had the school up at Bayou

George and that I was an honest person. I knew I had to scotch those rumors, because if people talked bad about a teacher, they could fire her. I told the sheriff about it, and he said, "Well, I'll fix it. Don't worry about it."

He came over from Panama City and said to Mrs. Robinson, "I understand that you have been telling lies about the teacher. They didn't have a school up here for years. Now they have a school for these young folks, and you are going to take the school out by telling lies about the teacher. If you keep doing that, we will put you in jail for libel."

I was standing right there. He said, "Teacher, do you want me to arrest her for lying?"

I said, "No, I just want her to be warned. I'm going to have a meeting of the parents tomorrow night, and if she'll come there to the school and apologize for what she said, I'll accept it."

He asked her if she would do that, and she said, "Yes sir, yes sir, yes sir."

So we had the meeting, and she apologized and said, "Don't ever say anything about that teacher. She will put the police on you." That settled that, right to the teeth.

At that time I was around twenty-seven and was feeling the need for a husband. During that school year I had moved out of the Eddings place and was staying on the weekends in Panama City with a woman named Wells who ran a café. I had told her that I thought I wanted to be married again. It was not like it is now; I always had this old-fashioned thing that without marriage sex wasn't right. If it had been the way it is now, I wouldn't have been thinking about a husband, but just about a companion or someone to satisfy my sex needs, and that would have been it. There weren't going to be any more children for me, because the doctor had told me I couldn't have any more.

During that time, Panama City was flourishing. People were moving in there, and industry was growing. People were just hunting for people to work for them; that's the reason that lady I met on the bus got me down there. A lot of women's husbands were making good money, and so the wives didn't want to do domestic work. Anybody with any business idea could have made money in Panama City at that time; I even did some hair, and I wasn't any hairdresser. When I think about it now, I wonder why women would come to me, but on Saturday, I'd have a room full of people, doing their hair for extra money. I doubt if it lasted until they got out of the door, but they were back there the next time.

Mrs. Wells said that people were talking about me and my friend Gussie, that they said we liked each other because we didn't have any boyfriends. That made me sick, and I said, "Well, that's a lie."

I told Gussie, "We're going to show them what we are." We started flirting with all the men, just leading them on, not meaning anything to any special one. Then they started talking about us again, saying we were whores and having every man in town.

After that, here comes a construction gang from Jacksonville, Florida. My landlady ran a café, an eating place, where these men ate. In this group of men was a tall, well-built, dark guy named James Myers from South Carolina, a smoothie if ever you saw one, just as congenial and pleasant. I had had this old fighting, mean husband, and this guy was just the opposite, so affectionate, everything a woman would want in a mate. He was so quiet and pleasant and considerate, that he made me feel like I was a paper doll. He had a kind of Geechie talk.

My landlady said, "You have been praying for a husband. That's the man for you. He seems so nice and religious." I kind of thought it might be, too, because I felt so comfortable with him. She just kept saying that I had been talking about getting a husband for a long time and that this man would make me a good husband. The job was about to be finished in Panama City, and the construction gang was going back to Jacksonville. James Myers had asked me to marry him.

I went home and talked to Mama about it. She said, "Well, if he's what you say he is, maybe he will make you a good husband."

I said, "But I'm supposed to go to summer school."

Mama had always told me that I was so progressive-minded that a man could hardly put up with me. She said, "Maybe that's your trouble; you are so independent and bossy. You need to let the man take care of you." I knew what I wanted and I didn't obey men, because I felt like I was equal and even more. I was smarter than the men I married, and I knew it and wasn't going to let them dominate me. Mama said, "Now when you marry this man, be a little more dependent; give him a chance to support you. You always work so hard, you act like you don't need their support and are self-sufficient. Sometimes a man wants somebody to lean on him." That was bad advice.

I was supposed to go to summer school that summer and have my teaching certificate updated. But no, I went up and bought some nice-looking lingerie and household things with the money I had saved to go to summer school with. In December of 1937, I came to Jacksonville and married James Myers. There was a minister there where he was rooming, and he married us. I wasn't going to stay with him unless we were married.

CHAPTER SIX

Settling in Jacksonville
(1937–1943)

In Jacksonville, I moved into James Myers's room on Beaver Street in a big old two-story house. But I kept asking him to get us a house. I didn't want to stay in a room. He'd say, "Well, we're going to get one, but we're going to get something real nice."

I said, "I don't care if it's a hut. I want something of my own." He never did anything about getting a house. Everybody in the house shared the kitchen and cooked on the same stove, and used the same bathroom.

The people I was around in Jacksonville were not my type of people at all—they weren't educated, they weren't Christian, they were just folks without any ambition or aspiration. They just worked and ate and lay up in the bed all day Sunday or drank liquor. I wasn't accustomed to that, so I stayed out of the way as much as I could. When my husband was on the job, I stayed in my room except when I went to the kitchen to fix the food. I stayed in there and read and slept. That was one time I felt I was really looking down on people; I knew I was better than they were. I was Miss "It."

But those people played nasty tricks on me all the time. I'd go into the kitchen and make a fire in the stove to cook my dinner on, a pot of peas or something, and then I'd go back to my room while they cooked, because I didn't stay around to go yakety-yak with those other women. When I would come back, my pot would be on the back, and their pots would be on the fire cooking. Or when I had hung clothes on the line, they would move them off the line and put theirs up. Things went on like that for six or seven months.

James Myers was as nice as he could be, for awhile, but then things changed. He had a girlfriend there in Jacksonville, somebody he had been with when he came to Panama City. She was looking for him to come back home where he was supposed to be. He told her some cock-and-bull story after he had come back and married me, but I think he slipped around with her anyway. In the meantime, he had recommended a good friend's wife as a hairdresser for me to go to. She knew all about this and filled me in about who this other woman was and that she was saying I wasn't married to him and that he was just making a fool out of me. I didn't pay too much attention, because I knew sometimes women get jealous and make things up.

But as the time drew on, and this was when the depression was coming on bad, one of his friends said, "James is not sociable at all on the job. He is always losing jobs because he just doesn't know how to get along with people. The boss man is always firing him, and he has worked for about every contractor in town." About a week later, he lost his job. When I asked him what happened, he said something or another about how the boss man had done wrong to him.

He fooled me too, lied to me, by telling me he was a cement finisher. That's above the mortar-mixer and makes a better salary. James Myers was a mortar-mixer, but that wouldn't have made any difference to me, or if he had just been the guy who carried the bricks if I loved him. Those lies started bad things building up, one after another.

The friend came by the house and said, "I told you. The boss man told James to do something or another, and James said he wasn't supposed to do that. The man said, 'Well, I'm asking you to do that now. You don't have anything to do right now.' James just said again that he didn't have to do it." Sometimes just to hold your job and try to live, you have to put up with a heap of things. I asked him whether he couldn't have gone on and done what the man asked him to do. No.

The next day I asked him for some money to get some food. I had to buy food every two or three days, because we didn't have a refrigerator or anything to keep food in. He said, "I don't have any job."

I said, "I know, but how do you suppose we are going to survive? You don't have a job, and I'm not working." I really didn't have any common sense. I could have gone to the school board and probably got a sub job. So I'm sitting up there playing cute and hungry. I told him, "Maybe if you weren't trying to take care of two families . . ."

He said, "What do you mean?"

I even called the woman's name. He just about went crazy, he was so mad. He said, "I'm going to slap you from . . . That's one thing I don't like for women to do, go around talking behind my back." He grabbed my hand, and I reached back there and got the knife on the dresser that we used to cut toenails, and I stuck it in his hand. He hollered, and then he went off and stayed away that night.

I had to start back to work. If I had had common sense or wisdom at that time, I would have gone to the school board and showed my old certificate and tried to get a temporary one, but nobody had enough intelligence to help me, so I just sat there and deteriorated. When hunger came, I remembered what Mama said, that it's not a disgrace to work for a living. I saw other people going out in the morning, women as old as I am now, going to catch the bus and go to work. I always felt like I could do what any other woman could do, so I asked the landlady if she knew anybody that wanted somebody to do domestic work. I hated to have to ask her, because here I had been the queen of Sheba, better than the rest of them in the house. She was glad that this old hussy was going to get a job, and she said, "No, but I'll sure look out."

I got a job the very next week, for a lady named Mrs. Livesey, who was from the wealthy Pace family that lived out on the river. Her parents had several servants, but she married a poor boy from a well-known family with no money but with a respectable name. This was during the depression, when money was really down low. She had a cute little house on Fitch Street where I went to work. That lady was a hard lady to work for. When I got home from work, my feet hurt so bad that I couldn't stand for a sheet to touch them. Still, I saw those other people going to work every day, and I thought, "If they can do it, I can do it." It was a consolation. I was making five dollars a week and carfare.

I didn't know how to do anything like working for people, except for the little work I had done as a child. In Panama City I had had a dream job, because the Wellses had a big beautiful house with a lot of big rooms we only went into once in a while. The only things I had to do there were downstairs. We kept that living room perfect, and the dining area, and the kitchen. We cooked together, and sometimes she would just want to cook by herself. I did the laundry, but it was easier than working in my own house.

But here in Jacksonville I went on this job where there were children, where I had to babysit, do laundry, scrub the woodwork, and get down and scrub and wax the floor with my hands. At Mrs. Wells', I didn't do the windows; a man came and did that. But here I was, doing windows, washing and ironing, cooking three meals a day, rubbing Mrs. Livesey's back every day, and taking care of her little boy.

Although the Liveseys didn't have any money, they were still associating with millionaires. Only once a week could they afford to have meat. They would entertain some of their fancy friends, and I would have to serve finger bowls with a flower petal in each one. The menu would be lima beans, white bacon, corn bread, and applesauce . . . and all this daintiness with that kind of food. On Saturday night we lived scrumptiously—we had meatballs. She had a way of making them called Swedish meatballs, with nutmeg in them. A friend of her husband's, Judge Lucky, came for dinner one night. He wasn't a judge then, but he was a young attorney who later became a well-known judge. She got her mother's butler to serve the food. There he was in uniform, serving meatballs at the table. After everyone had been served, she said, "May we have some more meatballs?"

The butler said, "Sarah says that's all there was."

"Well, may we have some more of the vegetables?" she said.

"That's all gone, too," said the butler. That was embarrassing! I was out there in the kitchen, just dying laughing.

Then Mr. Lucky said, "May I have a glass of water?"

The butler said, "That I can give you!"

If they had a chop, they just had one chop, and I didn't get a chop or a blop or a strip of bacon. That didn't bother me, because I would always go home, where I had me a little something to stir up, and it tasted good.

Their little boy Joe was spoiled. When I got my food, which was a very small amount, he would spit in it. I worked for the Liveseys until he spit in my food for the third time. When I complained to his mother, she said, "But he doesn't have any disease."

I said, "I don't care what he doesn't have. The next time he spits in my food, I might hurt him, and I think the best thing for me to do is to go. I could get myself involved in a lot of trouble. The next time he spits in my food, I'm going to slap the hell out of him." I left that job.

With all the badness that was going on between blacks and whites, my family always came out with respect, because we didn't beg people. We offered to work for what we got and to go beyond what was required of us to do. All we wanted to do was try to please. Then, if we did the best we could and we couldn't please, we womenfolks would just say, "Well, the Lord take it. If I can't please you, get somebody else." I have walked off jobs when I didn't have anything saved and didn't know where I would get the next penny. When I walked off from the Liveseys, after that boy spit in my food, I didn't know where I was going to get another job, but I wasn't going to work for a person who had a child like that and wouldn't chastise him. I wasn't going to have anybody spit in my food. I knew people who were mistreated and accepted it and didn't fight back because they were afraid. I never was afraid of any of those people, and yet I wasn't arrogant. I was kind, and I would do anything they asked me to do. I never said, "That's not my job." The way you treat other people is the way they will treat you. I think of that Scripture, "As a man soweth, so shall he reap."

As you get older, you learn to accept whatever condition you find yourself in. All of us have to die, with different things, but death is death regardless of whether a car hits me, whether somebody shoots me or somebody cuts me, whether I swallow poison or drown or have a disease take over my body. I don't have any control over that. So what I do, I do the best I can with what I have. As you grow older, you learn to be grateful that you have sense enough to know what condition you are in. It could always be worse.

One time when I was still with James Myers, I had fifty cents to get groceries with. I went down on Davis Street from Beaver Street where we lived. The bottoms of my shoes had worn out, and it was raining and flooding the streets with dirt and trash. A woman passed me in a pretty car, driving slowly in the traffic. I could see her face well, and it looked like she had razor cuts on it, and her hand was hanging out of the car with beautiful rings on it. She was cursing because the people in front of her wouldn't move.

I said to myself and to God at the same time, "Here I am, trying to be a Christian and good. And here you let this woman have this pretty car and pretty rings, and I don't have anything." I was young then.

When I got to the corner of Beaver and Davis, there was a man with both of his legs off, sitting on a kind of skateboard thing that he rode around on by pushing with his hands. His hands looked like gator tails, they were so rough, but he was smiling. The rain just beat down on him, and he was smiling. As I got ready to go into the store, there was a blind lady shaking a cup, dirty too and standing in the rain. It seemed like a voice spoke to me and said, "Sarah, you've got your eyes, and you've got your feet." I started praising the Lord right there in the street. I realized then that there's always somebody worse off than the other ones, and you should be thankful for what you have. I was standing up there crying, and people were looking at me. With my tore-up shoes and no money but fifty cents, I was still all right. I went in there and got my groceries and walked proudly back up the street home.

From that day on, I learned to be thankful for what I had, because a lot of people have got money and power and are not happy. Recently I thought of those two ousted dictators, Marcos from the Philippines and Baby Doc Duvalier from Haiti, with all the money and power they had, and now nobody wants them to stay in their country.

In the meantime Lib had moved down to Jacksonville with James David and was rooming with the people right next door to me and James Myers. When James David was about nine years old, Lib wrote me and said, "James is fooling Mama to death. He's getting into all kinds of little trouble, and Mama believes everything he says. I think he needs to be with you." I wrote Mama, without telling her what Lib had said, and told her that I thought it was about time for James to come and let me assume my responsibility as a mother.

Lib brought James with her when Mama let her come down to

Jacksonville to learn a trade. At first James got along fine. My husband and I were still rooming in a house, but I was determined to have a place of my own. Things were not going so well between me and James Myers, as I said before. I told Lib, "I'm going to move. I'm going to find a house. Would you be willing to move in with me?" She said yes, because she was tired of staying in a room too. She had to sleep with a girl she didn't like.

I found a little house for two dollars and a quarter a week, on Davis Street. We could manage that, with both of us working. There were four neat little old houses all in a row, right in front of a church. Our house was behind them, a neat little gray house trimmed in white and sitting back in a little alley. All those little houses were alike. The houses on Davis Street were a quarter a week more than mine. We had two rooms and a kitchen. You came in by the front bedroom, and went from there through a door to the next bedroom, and through that to the kitchen.

Davis Street had some trees and some old houses, and down below was an old junk store, run by a man named Roberts. The children would go there and buy candy. This was between Fifth and Eighth streets. It was within walking distance from the Duval Medical Center, that has become University Hospital now. It was two blocks from Cookman School, the elementary school. The bus ran right by my house. It was very convenient for me, but I didn't have any lights, and the only running water I had was on the back porch. The outhouse was in the backyard.

We moved in, but I didn't have any furniture or any household things. The people I was working for told me about a secondhand store, where I went and got a bed for a dollar and a half, and the man threw in one or two chairs. We got another bed for Lib. Somebody gave me an old stove, a wood stove, and we got an extra mattress. A friend of mine had been given some old things by the people she worked for, and she said I could have them if I would come and get them—a settee we made into a bed for James David. We were getting along just fine.

I told James Myers, "I have gotten me a house. If you want to come, you can. If you don't, you stay here." He said he wasn't going, and I said okay. About two weeks after we got there, here he came. I said, "Well, if you are going to stay with us, we're going to have to have another bed." He went to some furniture place and got one. There were just folks out in trucks peddling furniture. I guess black folks are the most furniture buyers that you ever saw, always changing furniture to get the new styles. They don't realize that the old stuff is the best. Now I think they're getting a little bit better and realize that all this stuff made out of plastic and glue doesn't last long.

I made a bargain with James Myers. I said, "I will take care of the food with the money I'm making, and you take care of the rent and pay the insurance." That was agreed. We were renting from Samuel C. Taylor, who was a ruthless landlord. He would put your furniture out in the street in a minute and let it rain on it if you didn't pay the rent. About three weeks after James Myers moved in, the insurance man came and said if I missed another payment, I would lose my insurance. It wasn't but a quarter a week. Then I got home from work one day, and there was a note in the door saying the rent man was going to put us out. James hadn't paid either one in two weeks. And he hadn't paid the bill on the cookstove. He was making twelve dollars a week, twice as much as mine, and here I was buying the food, and he was sitting up there eating my food. When he came in that night, I approached him with all this information and said, "Why haven't you paid the rent? Why haven't you paid the insurance? We are about to lose out in everything, and I've been keeping my bargain. I've been buying food, and you've been eating scrumptiously." He said he had to send his mama some money in South Carolina. I told him, "Your first commitment is to me. I don't mind your sending your mama anything. I think you should help her if she's in need, but you made a promise to me, and you haven't kept it. You still could have sent your mama some money and had enough to pay this little rent." I was fed up. I said, "Let me tell you something. You go to South Carolina and stay with your mama. Make up your mind what you want to do. When I get back here from my work, I want to see a receipt that you have paid the money on this house, or you have your clothes and go. If I have to do it by myself, you are not going to be here eating up my food."

When I got back home, he had taken his clothes and gone. I really cried. I said, "I have messed up my life. Two husbands." I was always taught that you married one man and stayed with him until he died. And here I was, married twice to two sorry men, out there struggling, with all my education gone down the drain because of them. I could still have been teaching. I said, "Lord, have mercy," prayed and cried. It wasn't because I missed him and loved him; I was just so disgusted. I said, "Well, that ends that for me. I'll never marry another man as long as I live. I've been taken advantage of, and now I'm going to take advantage of every sucker I find."

I went to the people I was working for, borrowed the money to pay the rent, and I went to Sears or wherever I had bought the cookstove, and got some leeway from them. I finally caught up with the insurance, with Lib's help.

That's what happened with James Myers. I never met any of his family, because times were too tough for us to go visiting. He married again, and I think he still lives in Jacksonville. I have seen him on occasion and spoken to him.

Here were these nice men back in Alabama who wanted to marry me, and instead I married those two Jims. I think I married for the wrong reason; I think sex had a lot to do with it. I wasn't familiar with sex, was afraid to do that unmarried. As a result, I got married so I could have it, and this is the person I want to have it with. Now that I can recall my reactions, that's really what it was, because James Hayes turned me on. Earlier than two weeks after marrying him, I wished I hadn't. It wasn't what I thought it was, didn't live up to my expectations, and I wanted to go home. He was only nineteen and didn't know how to handle any wife.

Another girl from Eufala named Lucy Coats moved into our little house after James Myers left, and that made it easier for Lib and me to make it. Back in Eufala, Lucy Coats had kept a little kindergarten and had been James David's first teacher. She was very nice but kind of strange and homely, skinny and black with long hair. Lib and Lucy shared a room, and she stayed for about a year.

Around that time, James David started taking money out of my pocketbook. That hurt me so bad. I would scold him and tell him how wrong it was and tell him not to ever do it anymore. Then he would go and do it again. I got me a switch, and I whipped the blood out of him, but that didn't stop him.

I went out and called a policeman off the beat and talked to him. I said, "I have a son I'm trying to raise, and I have whipped him and done everything I could think of, but he doesn't seem to take heed to it. Could you scare him for me? Maybe fright will do him good." He said he'd be glad to. He came in off the street and told James what he'd do to him if he caught him stealing. Said they would send him up for life, but that didn't do any good. Lucy Coats was still staying with me, and she had missed some money. I knew then that he was spreading out from me and had started messing with other people. One day I came from work, and by then I was living in a little house for two dollars and a half a week, and I had my rent money with me. There was a note in my door, written by James David, saying "There's a thief going around the neighborhood stealing folks' pocketbooks. He stole your pocketbook and threw it across the fence." Here that boy was trying to be so clever, but he never thought that I could recognize his handwriting. Besides, the note sounded like a child.

I looked in my room, and the pocketbook was gone, so I said to James David, "Let's go see if the pocketbook is over across the fence." There it was. I told him I knew he had done it, and he said some big boys made him do it.

I had heard about the boys' home, out here on Jesse Street. I went to the courthouse, to the Juvenile Department, and asked to see somebody about James. I said, "Now, I don't want to send him to Marianna [the state reform school] or anyplace like that, but I need some help. I have to work to support him." There wasn't any of that welfare stuff back then, and I wouldn't have been on it if there had been. My mama *never* went on it, even though we really could have used it. Even after that, during the depression, when she worked for some of the administrators of the government food-giveaway programs, those administrators were eating it. The only time she got any was when she fixed it for their dinner and there was some left over and they gave it to her.

In the courthouse, they gave me a slip that would admit James David to the boys' home. I went home and got James, and carried him to Jesse Street. He didn't know what was happening. I told him, "You're my oldest, and you're my youngest, and you're my onliest, and I love you more than I do anybody in the world. But I have to chastise you, or you are going to hurt me worse than you are hurting me now for taking my money."

We got him in there late that afternoon. I told the administrator, who was black, what the problem was. He said, "How long do you want him to stay?"

I said, "Just as long as it takes until you think he's not stealing. I love him, but I can't stand any rogues."

He ran away from there. One morning I woke up, and he was knocking on my bedroom window, crying. He said they were mean to him out there. I got up and said through the window, "Okay, just a minute." I put on my clothes and got him by the hand, and we caught the bus and went straight back out there. That showed that either I was a fool or had a hard heart or really intended to do what was right.

Lib broke down and cried and said, "Sarah, you are too hard." A lot of mothers would have just broken down, but I knew that I didn't want him coming up any rogue. It hurt me too, but I wasn't going to let him see any softness. I had lied and told my friends that he was at home in Alabama with my mother.

I would go out to visit him, and when Easter came, I carried Easter eggs for the boys, and I would carry cakes out there for them. As time went on, I got to be very friendly with the administrator of the place, and one day I got a letter from him, telling me, "I think James is doing pretty well, and it is just about the time now that I would recommend that he come home."

I went out there and I talked with him. I said, "If this is what you think, I want him home. I never did want him out here, but I just didn't want him to bother my things and other people's things."

They let him out, and I could send him in for my pocketbook, and he wouldn't take a thing. He didn't even want to go in there; he'd want to bring it to me and let me take the money out. But I'd say, "I want you to go in there and bring me a quarter." He'd go in there and bring it to me. I was able to trust him from then on.

James told me after he grew up, "Mother, I thought you didn't love me, but that was the best thing that you did for me." I worked and scuffled, had to put James David in the boys' home, but he came out pure gold.

The job I got after the Liveseys was part time, with Mrs. Thompson, across the street from where Lib was working. The Thompsons had two children: a boy about eight and a half they called Punky, whose real name was Clay Thompson, Jr., and a baby girl named Helen. I would get to her house in the morning before seven o'clock and fix their breakfast. I did the washing and ironing. Before I left at three o'clock, I would have cleaned the house, washed and ironed, cooked the dinner, and set the table. All Mrs. Thompson had to do was heat up the food and serve it. I would do that every day. Saturday I would come in the afternoon, after working for a Mrs. Lomax in the morning, and I would stay half the night while Mr. and Mrs. Thompson went out.

In those days we washed by hand, with coal pots, in a tin tub. A coal pot is a high kind of thing that you burn charcoal in. People used to put irons on them and heat them up so they could do their ironing. The coal pot was outdoors, and you put charcoal in it and put the tin tub on top and boiled the clothes. They didn't have polyester stuff then; everything was cotton and needed ironing. Even their little boy's pants were starched and ironed and creased.

Mrs. Thompson would go downtown and stay late some days. One time when Mrs. Thompson went off to town and stayed past the time I was supposed to go home, I finally got home and my next-door neighbor said that James David was begging bread. That hurt me so! I didn't leave food done for him, because the other children would come in and help him eat it. I didn't have that kind of money, to be feeding all the children in the neighborhood. But if I knew I was going to be late, I would fix something extra for him.

The next day, I told Mrs. Thompson about that and asked her to let me know ahead of time, the day before, if she was going to be late, so I could prepare something for James David. She went right on back to town, and by three o'clock she hadn't come. I had everything ready. I had given their little baby girl Helen a bath and had washed and rolled her hair. Everything was in order. I asked Mrs. Thompson's next-door neighbor to watch Punky, and Helen. That boy was just as dependable as he could be, and he's that kind of a man now. I didn't have to worry about him. I told the neighbor that I had to go home and see about my child, and I left.

Lib came home later with a note from Mrs. Thompson, cussing me out for leaving her children. She said they could have caught on fire and that I was no good and that she was going to tell her husband about this. That note was on a big, wide sheet of paper, and I turned it over and answered her. Lib said, "I'm not going to carry that note!" But I said, "You brought it to me, so you're going to carry it back."

I told that woman, "I love your children. I have worked and taken care of them, but I asked you to let me know when you got ready to go off and stay late. Tell your husband, if you want to, that I wasn't there. And while you're telling him that, tell him why you weren't home at the time for me to go. Send me my money. And I want you to know that your two children have you and their father and me to see after them, but my boy doesn't have anybody but me. And I love him just as much as you do your two."

Lib carried that note back. Then Mrs. Thompson started calling me when I was working at another lady's house, where I went sometimes to scrub the floors. Mrs. Thompson said she wanted to talk to me. I said, "There's nothing to talk about. I'll come back to you on one condition. I don't want to ever hear about this again." She said she was sorry, and I said, "Well, okay, I don't want to hear any more about it. I'm finished with it. You told me how you felt, and I told you how I felt. You know we understand each other."

They were my best friends. Around this time, when James David was in the fourth grade, he wanted a red wagon, and I was working for five dollars a week and carfare. I had to pay my rent out of it and my little insurance. The red wagon didn't cost any more than about three dollars, but I couldn't afford even that. I told the Thompsons about that. At home I told James, "I would get you anything like any other child would have, if I had the money, but I don't have it." I showed him what I made every week and how much I had to pay for each thing. I had to pay two dollars and a half a week for the house, but Lib helped with that. Then I had fifty cents for insurance. The two dollars I had left was for food. When that little ten-year-old boy saw that, he got a shoe box and went shining shoes. Right now, even though he's retired, he keeps busy. He doesn't mind working.

Then Christmas came along, and the Thompsons bought a secondhand bicycle for their boy, and a brand-new red wagon for James David. They are my friends to this day. Whenever I see them, we are hugging and squeezing and going on. The little girl was three months old when I first started working there. She would cry when I got ready to leave to go home, and want to kiss me. They were kind of embarrassed about it at first, and I saw that, so I tried to stay out of that. One day they had some company, and the little girl cried, "I want to kiss Byra." That's what she called me. I just threw her a kiss and started out. She slammed down and ran to me and put her arms around me and cried, "Kiss me, Byra, kiss me!"

Her mother said, "Well, she just loves Sarah so. It's not that way with every maid of ours."

I was the only maid they had, and one day I said, "You're not able to pay me. You need this money for yourself." She had one slip, and I had darned it for her, not one or two times. It was all darned up. But she was satisfied. With the money she was giving me, she could have had some pretty slips and cooked her own dinner and done her own wash. But no, she said she would rather have me.

Her husband was a good man. His father had been in the cigar business, and the business had gone under so that he had to help support his parents. They were wonderful people, and I hear every Christmas from those two children, Punky and Helen, and sometimes in between. Punky lives in Tampa, and Helen lives somewhere in California.

James David was always trying to do things to help me. He would go out and shine shoes on the streets and bring the money to me, to help out. One day when I came home from work, the kitchen floor was all white-looking. He had scrubbed that floor with Bon Ami. But he was looking out for his mama, and he has always been like that. As far as talking back, what the old folks called sassing, he never did that. He was always respectful and everything like that.

Then my niece Portia came to live with us, and she put James David out one day. She was clean and neat as a pin, always keeping her things darned and washed and ironed. Because she had a half-day job, she would be home before I would, and that day she and James had gotten to arguing about something, so she put him out. When I got home, he was sitting out by the fence, and he told me Portia wouldn't let him go in the house. I went in and asked what had happened. She told me about some little thing, but I said, "Wait a minute. This is the only home he has got. He's at home when he's at this house. I am the one who pays rent on it. Nobody puts him out unless it's me. Your home is in Geneva, Alabama. If you can't stand James David in this house, then you can go back to Geneva." She broke down and cried, but that was the end of that.

One time I sent James David back to visit with his father. After all, he needed his father and was crazy about him. James Hayes had a farm in Clio, and James David went up there. I had to write and tell Jim to send him home so he could go to school. When he came home, all his clothes looked like they had been washed in mud, what was left of them. Not a penny did Jim send me, not one thing did he buy him. I wrote and told him, "This is the last time that James David will come to see you. He's your child that you say you love, and yet you didn't think enough of him to even buy him a pair of pants." And James David had worked up there on the farm for his father. He didn't want to go back up there again, either. So he didn't see his father again until after he was grown.

In school, the boys would always beat James David up. He was small, and the big boys would always jump on him. He was growing, though, and gradually he got to be a big boy. Late one night when James was in the ninth grade, a man came to my house, knocking on my door, and asked me if I was James David's mother. I said yes. He had a tall boy with him, and he said, "Well, your boy jumped on my boy and beat him up, and I want you to do something about it."

I said, "Now, my boy has gotten beaten up a lot of times, and I have never gone to a parent yet. I told him to defend himself if he could, but if he couldn't defend himself, to run."

Now that old boy was about six feet tall, and I called James David and got him up out of the bed. He only came up to that other boy's chin. That man said, "Is that the one that beat you up?"

The boy said, "Yes sir."

That man cussed and said to his son, "You come on here. I ought to beat the hell out of you myself. You ought to live next to a skunk!" Here that boy went crying to his daddy, and when his daddy saw that peewee who did it come outside, he got mad at his son.

About that time my baby sister Catherine died. She had gotten married up in Eufala, when she was only seventeen or eighteen. She married David Frost. He built them a cute little old house sitting up on a hill, with a lot of rocks around it. She planted a running rose bush, and that bush is still growing. But Baby didn't live too long after she got married. She died at the age of twenty-two. Her first child was a little boy, and everything seemed to go well. But he got so that he couldn't walk. He had something like multiple sclerosis, although they didn't know what it was back then. Then Catherine had a baby girl named Helen. When Helen was born, some of those traveling nurses were going through the countryside, and they tested Catherine's blood. Because of the baby just being born, it was all mixed up, so they started giving her shots that ate up her liver. She died from that. If they had left her alone, she might have been all right. That was about 1944.

Lib was married by this time but was staying with Mama because the war had started by then and her husband was overseas. Mama and Lib raised Helen, and when Lib moved back down to Florida when the war was over, Helen was about three years old. When Mama moved down to Jacksonville later on, she brought Helen. Her daddy would get upset and send for her, but then after a while, she'd come back down here. So she went backwards and forwards, but she grew up mostly in Jacksonville and is still here.

During the time I lived on Davis Street, I had one dress, a Sunday dress, a black one. I never forgot my church, Saint Paul's, and I went every Sunday. Mama and Papa had told us that wherever we went, the first place to find friends and the good people in the community was the church. There are plenty of bad ones there too, but they are better than the ones who don't go at all. So I always did that.

At Saint Paul's I was in the Christian Endeavor League and sang in the choir at the night service. I couldn't go to morning worship, because I was working and had to fix dinner for the people I worked for. But I could go to the league in the afternoon and to the night service.

One time I was singing in the choir, sitting in a chair right behind the minister, who was a sweet man with a soft voice. I went to sleep and fell out of the chair. The people thought I was overcome with the Holy Spirit. I was so embarrassed that I let them go on thinking that, but I went back in the choir room and took off my robe and tore off home to Davis Street. I said, "Never, never, never."

The minister knew what had happened, and one time he said, "Sister, why do you always have to sleep?" I laughed and looked at him and said, "You know one thing? Your messages are so soothing." He just laughed.

Dudson, the president of our Christian Endeavor League, was semi-retarded, but he was so faithful that he was elected. I was very active in that and would help keep him pushed up. The conference came to Jacksonville, and the Sunday School State Congress was at Edward Waters College. The pastor came to me and said, "Dudson was supposed to be programmed to be on a panel discussion, but you know he can't do it. I want you to do it."

I said, "But I'm not the president."

He said, "That's all right; I want you to represent Saint Paul's." I told him I would, and I sat down and wrote it all out.

When it was time for me to get off work, it looked like the people I was working for just weren't going to get up from the supper table that night. They just sat there and talked. I had told them the week before that I wanted to get off as early as I could that night because I had to go to my church activity, and they had promised. I had to catch the bus from out in Riverside and come downtown. When I got off, I ran to the bus stop. At nighttime, you can hardly tell whether a person is black or white in a car. A car came by, and I waved this guy down. He turned out to be a white person, but they brought me to town. I was working with the PTA at that time, and this person was PTA folks too, so we got to talking about that as they brought me to town. When I got to town, I had to catch a bus, because I had to transfer down on Bay Street. While I was waiting there for a bus to go to Davis Street, this tall-looking, nasty-looking white man came up and started harassing me, saying ugly things. I said, "I'm going down here and talk to this policeman about you."

I walked down there and told the policeman, but he said, "He doesn't want you."

I said, "Well, thank you. Maybe he doesn't, but I've got your number. My boss man works with Sheriff Rex Sweat."

He said, "Oh, well, I'll come and see about him. He's not going to bother you."

When the bus came, I had lost my transfer. I had just one more token to go to work with the next day. There were lots of transfers and pieces of paper all around the bus stop, so I picked up one of them. It was a day-old transfer, and I was digging in my pocketbook, looking for my transfer. The bus driver said, "Lady, I'm going to have to put you off." So I had to give my last token.

I was frustrated when I got home. I didn't have time to bathe or anything. I just put my one black dress over my head and tore out for Edward Waters College. Fortunately I had a friend who had an old piece of car and stayed next door. I got him to carry me out there. When I got there, the people were all there; my pastor was sitting up there looking. When he saw me come in, he beckoned for me to come to the platform. There was the bishop sitting up there on that platform. I could hardly walk. I don't usually get nervous, but I was shaking. I would try to cross my legs, and they wouldn't stay crossed because I was shaking so. Fortunately I was the last one to speak, so I had a chance to cool off. We were all speaking on the same subject, so I was able to pick up some ideas from what the others said, and enlarge on them in my own way. But if they hadn't had a pulpit up there to lean on, I think I would have just squashed down there on the floor.

When my time came, I got myself kind of composed. I looked around, and the auditorium was full. The sky just opened up for me just like it did for my high school oration. I didn't even look at my paper. My pastor was really happy and said I was the best one. So I got over that, but it liked to have done me in, tired and sweaty.

I was having a hard time around then, working hard but just getting by. At that time I had two jobs. I was working five days a week for the Thompsons, and they didn't have much either. They paid me three dollars and a half a week. Then on Saturday morning I worked for the Lomaxes scrubbing and cleaning up her kitchen, for about seventy-five cents.

Mrs. Lomax was a dressmaker who lived in a pretty good neighborhood, but she and her husband were just kind of common people. He had a good, steady job working on the railroad, and she did beautiful sewing. She was a good cook, a soul-food cook, and she liked to cook up big pots of things. She would always give me a big lard bucket of something like cabbage and pot liquor with meat in it to carry home. When I got home, I just cooked some bread, and that was our dinner.

Saturday afternoons, after I finished at the Lomaxes, I went over and worked at the Thompsons'. I would usually stay at night so they could go out on the town. It would be twelve o'clock sometimes when they got back, but I would make them carry me home anyway. They'd come in there and be kind of half out of it, but I figured that if they rode high and got there safely, they could take me home.

I had one black dress for Sunday and would wear it plain one Sunday and with an embroidered collar the next. Then Mrs. Lomax had given me a bunch of artificial violets, and I would wear them the next Sunday. One time Lib did go with me and I got another dress for two ninety-eight; oh, boy, that was a knockout, I thought—a change from old blackie. But not having nice clothes didn't stop me from going to church. I told the pastor that I really didn't have enough money to give to the church like I should, and I felt like I shouldn't go. He said, "Oh, no, you come on. You give service. A lot of people give money but they don't give service. You give your service, and one day the Lord will bless you and you will be able to give money. You know you have to live and take care of your child, so don't worry about it." Sure enough, that's what happened.

When James David was sixteen, he told me he wanted to go into the service. He said that he wanted to get in the navy, where he could help me. This was before he finished high school. I told him, "No, you're too young. You don't know what you're doing."

He insisted and said, "If you don't let me get in the navy, I'm going to run away."

I said to myself, "Well, Lord, maybe he's trying to say something to me." I let him get in the navy. Now he was only sixteen, so he lied and said he was seventeen. I went along with it, but I told him, "Now I'm not saying you're that age, but I'm not disputing it. If anything comes up, I'm going to be involved in it, because I'm permitting you to do it."

"There isn't going to be anything," he said.

Two weeks after he got in there, a neighbor two blocks down the street, who ran a funeral home, called me and said they had a long-distance call from Chicago. We all knew each other in the neighborhood, and they had a phone. I went to the phone, and there James David was, crying, telling me to get him out. I told him, "I didn't want you to get in. You thought you were man enough, and now you're going to have to really prove that you're man enough. I will not get you out."

I wrote the chaplain a letter and told him that James was upset and that he had never been away from home by himself before. I told him that he was a good boy but maybe he was too young to go into the service, and I asked him please just to say a word to him. The chaplain did, and I didn't hear any more from that.

James stayed in the navy for three or six years. When he got out of that, he went back and joined the army. He married a lovely person who is a schoolteacher, and they had two children, Willie Fred and Lisa. And James stayed in the army until he retired.

CHAPTER SEVEN

Home on Castellano
(1947–1956)

When I was living at 1453 Davis Street, I was working for Mrs. Thompson. A low-income housing project was being built close to me, and I applied for a place in it. All indications had pointed towards me getting in a nice, new, clean house where I would have an electric stove and electric lights. From the time they started the project, I kept running down to the office to see when I could put in my application. When the time came, I wasn't making enough. I cried all that night, thinking that here I was, a poor person, yet I couldn't get a place to live in a project for poor folks. But I vowed that I was going out to the airbase in Orange Park, just south of town, and get a better-paying job, and I did it.

The war was going on by this time, and so they needed more people at the base. When I decided to go, my niece, Portia, was staying with me, and I told her I was going to the airbase and get a job, so I could earn enough to qualify for that housing project. Portia said they weren't hiring out there, because she had been out there the day before and couldn't get anything. I was determined, and I went out there and got a job that day, cleaning up around the engine-overhaul place. It seems to me that I must be led by the Holy Spirit, because when the need comes, I am there in the right place at the right time to receive help.

I would make my work pants. A lot of the girls were spending their money as they got it, buying slacks. Some of them were strutting around in high-heeled shoes, going to work. I didn't; I was saving my little nickels and dimes. I wanted a better life. I had two things in mind—to go back to school or to buy a place of my own. A girl told me about a lady who had lost her husband and was going to sell her little place out to the northwest of Jacksonville, just for pennies, so to speak. I resolved to move into that shack and build around it. But when I got there, some relative had come and claimed the place. I wasn't going to get involved in that kind of thing.

I had been to the agency out on Twenty-sixth Street that was selling lots out in the northwest area, and the man told me about a Jim Walter house. Jim Walter is a company that builds shells of houses and a roof, and you finish it off. You could get the house and the lot for sixteen hundred dollars, and I decided I would get it. What I asked myself was, "If I don't have the airbase job, can I pay twenty-five dollars a month?" And I said, "Yes, I could afford that on a regular job." I never believed in going over too big, losing everything.

In the meantime, where I lived the rent was frozen. I was paying two dollars and a half a week. Portia was staying with me, and I had one of the rooms rented out, and that room was paying my house rent. With the job at the airbase, I was doing pretty well. But my friends who had gotten houses in the low-income project were having trouble, because every time they got a raise, the rent would go up. I saved my little money all that time and came out here and bought a Jim Walter house right on this street, Castellano.

At this time, I hadn't divorced James Myers, and I didn't want him to have any claim on my house. So I told Lib about it and said, "I don't want to go through any divorce courts. You and I are going to buy this together, but you won't have to pay a penny. I just want you to cosign with me, to keep him from messing with it." She agreed, and we bought the house. I paid fifteen hundred dollars for the whole thing. I had saved up three hundred dollars down payment. The lot was one hundred by seventy-five feet, and it was muddy, on an unpaved street. But when I moved out here, I was so happy! I had saved up nearly four hundred dollars, so I had enough to buy some things to go in the house. Before that, I was still using all that old secondhand stuff I had scraped up for the Davis Street house; I hadn't bought a thing.

For the new house, I had to get materials to finish the walls, and a kerosene stove to cook with. It was March 1947 when I moved out here. There was one house between Moncrief and my house; it was mostly woods out here. My friends laughed and poked fun and said I was silly to move way out in the woods. Since that time, they have passed me and were glad to get way beyond me, farther from town.

By now, the street is paved, and I have lived on it, in this community, longer than I have lived anywhere else in my life. This is where I met Rice, the only real husband I had. After I came, my mother came to see me and liked it; she bought a lot and built herself a house. My baby brother was with her. Mama lived here until she passed, when she was seventy-two. Lib in the meantime got married, and she bought a lot out here. She lives on the next street. My brother J.D. was in the army and was going to live in Eufala when he retired, but he came to visit and liked Jacksonville, so he got a place on this street. So the only ones in our family that aren't here are Beatrice in Geneva and James in Nashville. Albert lived here too, for a while. Then he moved up to Akron, Ohio, and then to Columbus, Georgia, where he died.

When I moved out here, I had met a man in town who had an old-fashioned Dodge that was square like a house, a '23 Dodge or something like that. Everybody knew that car because it was almost antique. He was a drayman, and I got him to move my stuff out here in his truck.

He got excited about me, so I got him to build me a yard to put chickens in. As it turned out, I would just as soon have built it myself, because I had to be right there with him to hand him the nails and all the other materials. He was a little skinny, dark-skinned man who looked like a spider. They called him Grant. He told me that his wife had died and all about how lonely he was.

I went to his house one day, a neat little house. A fence was around it, with a lock. We went in the house, and it was locked, naturally. But every room in that house had a lock on it. The kitchen cabinet where he kept his groceries had a lock on it. The chickens were locked up in the chicken coop in the backyard. He showed me the dresser drawer where he kept his valuables—papers and things. It was locked up. I said, "How do you know what key to use to get into what?"

He came to see me for a few weeks until I got sick of him. I never did

tell him he could come; he just decided he was going to be my boyfriend.

After I had been in the house about two weeks, a hurricane came
and blew the top off. It rained all over the furniture. Here I was, not
knowing the people in the community, so I got a cab and went to his
house to ask him to put the tar-paper roof back on for me. He did come,
but Andrew Rice, who lived down the street with his wife, and Mr.
Shepherd, another neighbor, saw what had happened and came up and
helped put it on. Their wives told me, "You didn't have to go hunt
anybody else." That's the kind of people they were.

I said, "I'm a stranger here, and sometimes a woman has to be very,
very careful when she asks other women to let their husbands do
things for her. I'm glad you all volunteered. I appreciate it, but I never
would have asked you."

The first thing I did when I came out here was go to a church—
Philadelphia Baptist Church, right next to the cemetery. Somebody
had a hogpen close by, and I couldn't stand the odor. When they would
raise the windows in the summertime for air, in came the flies and in
came the odor from the hogpen, because there were no screens in the
windows. Even though the people in the church were very nice, I
didn't join.

Mama had visited me before, when I lived downtown, but when I
moved out to my own house, she fell in love with the community, and
she decided to buy a lot here. She didn't sell the homeplace in Alabama. She was a very conservative person and had saved up a little
money. The lot didn't cost but three hundred dollars. I was to get a
man to build a house on it. Lumber was hard to get at that time because of the war, so we used quite a bit of boxcar lumber, wood from
old boxcars that were torn up. The lumber was solid and seasoned.
The framework came from that and from old buildings that had been
torn down.

The man who I got to build it, who said he was a carpenter, was
named Mr. Frederick. He lived in this community. I didn't know how
to build a house, but I knew what it should look like. I told him that. I
would buy nails, and he would carry them home, because in the mean-

time he was working on his house too. He told me to get eighteen-foot two-by-fours, when he didn't need but fifteen feet. He would saw off three feet and waste that wood. I was right on his tail all the time; I knew what it ought to look like. I was working too, so I couldn't be there to watch him all day. Somebody really needed to be there to watch him. I let him frame it up and put a roof on it, and then all of us in the family got in there, even Helen, who was a little old girl, handed the boards up. We did the ceiling and the siding. The siding was that water resistant kind that looks like brick; we put that around it.

So Mama came to live in Jacksonville. Oh, what a blessing that was! She must have been around sixty-five or sixty-six, and that was about 1949. She lived here until 1955, when she died at the age of seventy-two. When she moved out here, we were all happy to have her. Lib was down here, and I was here. Beatrice was always visiting around, and she was a great writer. She could write the most interesting letters, and she wrote often. I always kept stationery in my house just for Beatrice. If she came to visit me, she would write letters to all her children, her sisters and brothers wherever they were.

Mama moved here, and she wanted a church home. There was a Methodist church out here a long time ago, where they had kept the school. But the church had burnt up, and they had never built it back, even though the conference still had it named as a church and kept the land. The man who ran the Two Spot Night Club gave them a plot of nice dry land down by the Two Spot, because the woods had grown over the land where the old church had been. It was kind of swampy, too. Mama was in on the building of the first new church. I moved my membership from the big church downtown, out to the little one. We had raised some money to get an old piano and fix up some things. Every Saturday, I would sell sandwiches and fried fish out in my back-yard for the church. I had one hundred and thirty dollars that I had raised that way. When annual conference time came, our pastor was assessed eighty dollars for his six members. The constitution said each church was to send two dollars for each member, so that made only twelve dollars. The eighty dollars included a heap of other stuff. The pastor thought he needed all the money I had raised, to pay off the eighty dollars and to pay his expenses for going to the conference. I told him he wasn't going to get it. My darling mother looked at me in the eye and said, "You know better than that. He is our pastor. I don't care if you did raise the money by selling fish, you raised it in the name of the church. The money belongs to the church, and the pastor is the chief executive of the church. He can order any treasury in the church to be used for church purposes. You are going to give him that money."

I gave it to him. But you can see, all down my line, how I act toward a challenge. Before I gave it to him, I went out to the college, where the bishop's office was, and asked the secretary if I could speak with him. She asked me if I had an appointment. I told her, "Ever since I was born, I had an appointment. I was born African Methodist Episcopal, and my daddy was a minister."

She looked at me, and I guess she said to herself, "I better let this fool talk to Bishop Greggs."

He said, "Sister, what can I do for you?"

I said, "I am a member of the little church that was named for you. We are proud of our name, but you are walking on little tender plants."

He said, "What are you talking about, Sister?"

I said, "When you have tender plants coming up, you have to be gentle with them, because if you walk on them, you will stunt them or break them down, and they won't grow. There are just a few of us out there. There are a lot of Baptists and Holiness, all kinds of denominations growing by leaps and bounds. We are just coming up. The constitution says our assessment should be two dollars from each member. We have six members and a few children, but our assessment is eighty dollars. Don't you think that's too much?"

He said, "The presiding elder recommends to me what each church can take up. He's out there, and every three months he checks on the membership. Now I will admit that sometimes they try to build their district up to make it look good for them."

I said, "Well, he really built us up."

He said, "Well, that really is too much. I tell you what I am going to do." He wrote out a check for thirty dollars and gave it to me and said, "Your church can put in the other fifty dollars. Next year it won't be like this."

I said, "Thank you, Bishop."

He said, "You are a fine woman."

When they had the business meeting at the church, the pastor wanted the eighty dollars, and I got up and turned fifty dollars over to him and the check from the bishop. He looked at the check and said, "What? Where did this come from? This has the bishop's name on it!"

I said, "The bishop gave it to me."

The pastor said, "Oh, my God!" He was a little young minister, and he didn't know where he stood. Here I was, had jumped up and gone to the head man. But that bishop died before the next conference, so he didn't get a chance to straighten that out. Still, I sure got that thirty dollars. I gave some of my fish and sandwich money to the pastor, too, to go to conference with.

I like to work for a cause, but I don't like to be taken advantage of. I respect leadership, and I will follow it, but I want to know why the leadership wants things from me. If a person can't explain his reasons, then I will question it. If I have the opportunity to go to that person privately, I will go to him privately and discuss it, rather than in front of an audience. But if I don't have any other time to do it, that's when I will do it.

Okay, Mama was here and working in the church. She showed her age more than I'm showing mine now, and I'm five years older than she was when she died. She took that little church to heart as if it was her baby, and she was nursing it. Her friend Mrs. Leach worked with her, though she didn't join the church because she was a Baptist. Mrs. Leach had a little finance that she donated to the church, and I think she gave us the piano.

I had another old boyfriend before I married Rice, who didn't like church or preachers or religion. He told me, "I don't want you going around and buying Cadillacs for these preachers."

I said, "Let me tell you one thing. The tree that's going to be made into a cradle that's going to rock the baby that's going to talk to me about not going to church—the acorn hasn't even been planted yet. You and nobody will ever stop me from going to church. If the preacher can take a quarter a week and buy a Cadillac, more power to him."

Then every Sunday, he started saying, "Put this in church for me," and would give me a little something.

That man was very jealous. My mama was living right up the street by that time. I had her and one of her old friends to come have dinner with me one Sunday, and he had come out to see me. Mama and Mrs. Leach were sitting there and laughing and talking. He said, "When are they going home?"

I said, "What did you say?"

He said, "When are they going home? I came to see you, and you have to entertain them."

I said, "They will leave whenever they get ready. That's my mama, and she can stay here all day if she wants to."

He had brought me some magazines to read, and some to send to James, who was in the service. He said, "Well, I just feel like taking my books and going."

I said, "Yes," and I grabbed a lamp. I went up beside his head, broke the lamp chimney on him. He was a dresser: wore the most beautiful shirts and was real neat. I got lamp oil all over him and a little blood, where the chimney kind of stuck in him.

He said, "You crazy?"

I said, "Get out of my house, and don't you *ever* come back." And I threw the books at him.

Mama heard it and came running, saying, "What's the matter? What's the matter? Don't you touch my child!"

He said, "She's the one on me!"

That guy took off across the field, cut through the cemetery, and got to a joint that he frequented. All of them knew him there, where they would shoot craps and drink. When he went in there, they said, "Some woman had hold of you!"

I was so mad, I didn't know what to do, at him trying to make me run Mama home. That was the end of him.

In the Jacksonville schools, the county provided the books, but the blacks only got the books the white schools had already used and discarded. When the blacks got them, they were already obsolete. The teachers had come through the same system, and so the black teachers were just as far behind as their students were. But in the black schools, what they studied, they learned. They were proud of their teachers, proud of their schools. And they have gone out of these schools, with the inadequate textbooks, and survived in the white schools. I think it's individual. You can go to the best schools in the world and have the finest teachers, and if you don't have it in your head and in your heart to learn, it won't happen.

Somehow or another I established myself in this community as a respectable woman, and the people found out that I didn't mind asking the right people for what I thought we deserved. Soon after I got out here, one of the teachers up here at the Moncrief Elementary School met me and said, "We need a PTA president. Would you serve?"

I told her, "No, I don't have any children going to school."

She said, "That doesn't matter. We need somebody, and I believe you would be good. I'm going to offer your name."

I said, "You can offer it if you want to, but I don't think I'd serve." She did, and I reluctantly accepted it. But I was glad I did. We had one of the best and the biggest PTAs in Duval County. That's what Mr. Ray Green said, who was our county commissioner at that time.

We had a beautiful new school, but hardly any equipment. The people were so proud because they had never had a schoolhouse built for them. Before that, they had had schools in churches. A one-teacher schoolroom was all they had, and all these children had to walk into town for high school. There were no buses in those days.

We got that PTA organized. I wasn't that smart, but it looked like things just revealed themselves to me, and I could get them to work. We had a lot of parents who were welfare participants; they weren't on welfare, but they could have been. Welfare wasn't as prevalent then as it is now. They were poor scufflers, scrambling for what they could get for their children. Then we had some people who were better off, doctors and teachers—the upper crust in our society—whose children were going to school there too.

I organized homeroom mothers. I hadn't heard of it before, but I just thought it was a good idea. Everyone liked it so well that we put two in each room. I would put a doctor or teacher's wife in with a poor working person's wife. I organized committees too, and each one had a mixture of the community in it. The poorer-class people were glad to be working with this supposed upper crust, and the upper crust were glad to have these others who would do more of the work. But they had a common goal, which was the good of the children. They didn't go every day, but they would keep tabs to see what the teachers' needs were and see how the children were getting along, let them know that they loved them. If the class needed pencils and paper for children who couldn't afford them, the homeroom mothers would provide, or notebooks and other such little things. Some children needed to be on the county free-lunch program, so the mothers would arrange that. If the children were eligible, but their eligibility had not yet been proven, the PTA saw to them getting a lunch. The PTA would even be in touch with the homes of the children. If there was a burnt-out family, for instance, or if there wasn't enough food there, we provided for that.

We gave so much a month to the PTA, and those funds were used for these purposes, plus there was a Duval County fee and a Florida State PTA Association fee. When those meetings came, we would take care of the expenses of our president or another representative to go and bring back information to our group.

The things we tried to get from the school board, we couldn't get, and when we had exhausted all our begging and going on to them and trying to show them the reason why we needed it, we went and got it ourselves. We bought an intercom system for our school, we decorated the teachers' lounge and bought milk for a woman with twin babies. We had a kind of a clothes bank, that got clothes up for the children who were coming to school without enough, and we followed through to see whether the parents were taking care of them. In the same way, we had a food bank.

We held one fund-raising event a year, and I decided one year that we would have a banquet for that purpose but that we would have to fix the food for ourselves. That banquet raised fifteen hundred dollars. People bought tickets for about two dollars to come to the banquet. We had turkey and dressing, mashed potatoes and peas. And guess who was in the kitchen to get the carcasses of the turkeys—the doctors' wives—to make soup.

There were other things we got by worrying the people downtown until they gave it to us: lights, playground equipment. I went to Mayor Burns about a traffic light we were trying to get on Forty-fifth and Moncrief. He sent me to another office; I went there and they gave me the runaround. Then I went to Commissioner Green, and then I went and I went and I went. Finally I think they said, "Give this fool what she wants." So we got the traffic light.

Although I had a boyfriend from time to time for companionship, there was never anything serious until I got to know Andrew Rice after his wife died. I had joined what we called a little civic saving club, the Triangle Club. Rice and his wife were members. It was made up of people in the community. One of the men who was a member was a minister, and he had a school bus. His wife was our president, and she would always suggest where we would have trips. We would go in their school bus and pay a certain amount to cover the expense. He was getting the money from driving us. It turned out that we weren't getting anything for our efforts in our little projects. By the time we paid him for riding in his school bus, we didn't have anything to give the concern.

The last thing they had was a fish fry down at New Berlin; we worked at that fish all day. We were to divide the proceeds among the club members who had worked at it. But that minister had brought everybody in his bus to the fish fry, and there weren't so very many people. Seventeen cents apiece is what we got, after we had paid him for driving his bus. I said, "That wasn't worth it. As far as I'm concerned, never count me in on a bus project. I'll take my seventeen cents out of my own money."

Finally the club busted up, but I had gotten to know Rice and his wife through the club. I hadn't had much time for visiting in the neighborhood, because I was working all the time. When I wasn't working at home, I was working at church or at the school. I liked Rice's wife Kitty, though; she was a sweet, kind of ignorant person, very neat and very clean, and she was an usher in the church. But she was an alcoholic.

I'd go over to visit with her sometimes, and we'd be having a conversation when Rice would come in and take the conversation away, "Blah, blah, blah." I couldn't stand that old flappy-trap Mr. Rice.

Kitty and Rice were having problems I think because of her drinking. Rice had a fantastic garden, full of fat tomatoes and string beans and every kind of vegetable you could want, that they canned. She said, "Rice won't buy me anything. He just wants me to eat string beans and potatoes and tomatoes that we raise, and I want other things."

I said, "Well, honey, you do days' work and get your pay every day. Your husband works at night, and when you come home from your work, you can stop by the store and buy yourself a little steak or pork chop and cook it for yourself. The scent of it will be gone by the time he comes home. Let him eat his vegetables."

She said, "A friend of mine said she'd quit him."

I said, "That friend of yours would be the first one standing in his door when you decided to come back and pick up something you had left. If that's the only thing bothering you, you stay with your husband. There's always a way out, if it's food that you're talking about. I wouldn't even worry about it. I'd have beans and things cooked for him, but I'd be sitting up there with a cow lowing in my stomach because I had used my money and had me a juicy steak." He didn't bother her money; she could do what she wanted with it.

Kitty had a drinking problem but would only drink on the weekends. Still, that made Rice feel terrible. He told me he married her because during the depression when he couldn't find any work, she took care of him. He was staying with his mama and walked all over town every day, trying to find work. One day he was plumb barefooted, and he said, "Lord, if I had three dollars, I could buy me a pair of shoes." He was ushering at his church and needed those shoes. His pants were about to give out too. He found three dollars and bought a pair of shoes. His mama had a job and thought he could find something, so she said, "I'm tired of taking care of you."

Kitty, who became his wife, had a job and would bring food from work and feed him. He loved her for that. She was a very homely-looking person and had had a hard time in her life. He married her, and his mother was torn up because she was a very proud woman and thought he had married beneath himself. Kitty turned out to be a life-saver for her, though, because she got sick and Kitty took care of her.

The doctor had told Kitty not to drink; she had some kind of small vessel in her heart. One Saturday night before the first Sunday in May, she got a blood clot in her heart and died. She was fifty-three or fifty-four. She and Rice had gone out to a little party that night, came home and went to bed. Miss Lula was staying with them, an old lady who had been living in the neighborhood. When she lost her husband and her mother, who looked younger than she did, she was afraid to stay in her house by herself and asked if she could stay with Rice and Kitty. She was a good cook too and had gotten up and was fixing breakfast.

Rice had plenty of chickens then and was selling eggs, and they kept the eggs in their room. Somebody came to buy a dozen eggs, so Miss Lula knocked on the door to wake them up. It was time for them to be up anyway; she had breakfast ready for them. Rice got up to get the eggs and saw what time it was and realized that it was late. He got the eggs for the customer and then went to wake Kitty up, but she didn't wake up. He said he shook her, and a funny feeling went through him. He called Miss Lula, and Miss Lula said, "I believe she's gone!" She had died in her sleep.

Miss Lula started screaming and going on, and she ran up to my house just up the street to get me to help. I was not home but was at my new little Methodist church, Greggs Temple. I was assistant to the pastor and had to raise all the hymns and teach the Sunday school. We only had six adult members and ten or fifteen children. My mama was really the boss, but I had a pretty good hand in there too.

Rice and Miss Lula sent around to the church to get me. That was like sending for the lawyer or the judge. I wasn't that close to them, but they respected me for some reason. When they came and got me out of church, he acted like I was his mama. His mother and sister were in town, but they hadn't gotten the word yet. I said, "I'm so sorry." He had to go downtown and notify the police and get the officers to come to his house and pronounce her dead. He asked me if I would go with him, and I told him I'd be glad to. Another lady was here by then, and she came too. They asked what kind of medicine she had been taking and when she had been to the doctor last, but he didn't know. But I had talked to her recently about doctors and things, so I answered the questions for him. I think he was just so upset that he didn't know what to say.

Kitty's aunt came to the funeral from Savannah, Georgia, and her sister came too from Coconut Grove near Miami. They stayed about two weeks with Rice. While they were here, the aunt said, "Now Rice, you are young enough that you need a wife. If you ever marry, try that little woman in the house over there. I believe she'd make you a good wife." Rice said later that it didn't sink in too much, but when Kitty's sister Blossom got ready to leave, she said, "That Sarah Myers up across the street is your wife. You call her and talk to her."

One time when he was fixing a door or something in my house, he had said to me, "If I was a single man, I sure would give somebody some trouble." I hadn't paid any attention, because he wasn't even my kind. I wasn't studying about any husband anyhow; I had made up my mind I would have a fling with somebody now and then, but when I got through with it, that was the end of it. I wasn't ever going to get messed up in a marriage again. Two times was enough; I knew the third time, I was out.

Rice called me on the phone and I asked who it was. "It's Rice," he said.

I said, "Yes sir, Mr. Rice, what can I do for you?"

He said, "I just called you to tell you I love you and want you for my wife."

I said, "You WHAT?" On the telephone! He asked if he could come to see me. I said, "Are you drunk? Mr. Rice, you must be drinking. You don't know what you are talking about. Your wife just died.

"There are plenty of women in this community and all over town that are single. Some of them would take advantage of you in the condition you're in. But I'm not going to do it. You let yourself get straightened out. Look around. Then after you look around at all these other women that are looking for a husband, if you still feel the same way, come and talk to me." I hung up.

I went down to Mama's house. I was so tickled, that I couldn't wait to tell Mama. She said, "What in the world is wrong with you?"

I said, "Mama, guess what happened. Old Rice called me up and told me he loved me and wanted me for his wife." One of Mama's old buddies, Mrs. Terry, was there, and she said, "If I was ten years younger, I'd marry him myself." If she had been ten years younger, she still would have been in her sixties. Rice was about forty-six.

Mama said, "What did you say?" I repeated it. She looked at me real seriously and said, "Rice is a good man. You need a husband! My suggestion to you would be to say yes."

Mama didn't laugh and all, and my laugh just kind of dried up. I started thinking seriously about it.

Lib's sister-in-law had one of her little nephews staying with her, named Toby. He was a typical little boy—big eyes, innocent and inquisitive. He'd come up to my house to visit me. Sometimes when Rice would come home from work, he'd stand in his yard and look up toward my house. Toby said one time, "Aunt Sarah, that man is looking up here. Do I have to go home?"

I said, "No." That little boy had sense enough to know that Rice was interested in me, and he didn't say anything about anybody else.

One day Rice walked up to my house and said, "Have you thought about what I said?"

I said, "Well, have you done what I suggested that you do?"

He said, "I'm looking."

I said, "Well, just keep on looking."

Rice carried me to work one day in his old truck named Charlie. It was an old T-model car cut down into a truck; it didn't have any doors, so you had to hold onto the seat to keep from flying out. I was running late. When my boss man saw that, he said, "That's going to be Sarah's husband."

One evening about four months after Kitty died, Rice came to my house, and it was the strangest thing that ever happened to me in my life. He just came walking up toward me, and it looked like I just melted away. I couldn't push him back, or do anything. It was just like a spell was on me. I reckon that was love. I was never the same anymore. He looked different; I felt different about him. I told him that after I got my divorce from James Myers, I would marry him. Judge Peeler granted that divorce.

In the meantime, Lib had married, and I had to get her name off my house deed before that husband would come in there too. The lawyer said that by her marrying, that gave her husband part of my house. I had to get Lib to sign a quitclaim deed. She and her husband weren't getting on too well. He was a kind of mean, cunning, sly guy, and I had to slip this thing in on him before he realized what was happening, or he wouldn't have signed it just for meanness' sake. I got him to sign it. I owed about one hundred dollars more on that house. Rice gave me the money to finish that off and get the title cleared.

It took some time to get my divorce straightened out. In the meantime, Rice's mama told him that it was too soon after Kitty's death for him to be thinking about marriage and to be courting. She and her daughter went down to his house one Sunday, and I was down there helping Miss Lula fix the dinner. She asked me what I was doing there and said, "Do you think you ought to be in this house?"

I said, "Yes, this is Rice's house and he invited me and I am engaged to be married to him. I am not a young girl; I am a grown woman. You and nobody else but Rice has the authority to question my being here." She smiled, and I didn't have any more problems with her at all. She respected me, and I got to be her friend. I don't shy around. I know who I am and what I want and where I'm going. If there's a problem to confront, get it over with, and love the people right on.

She started coming to his house, because I started cooking the whole thing. She would come around and eat and enjoy herself and want to know how long it was going to be before I got my divorce.

Before we got married, Rice was up at my mama's house and went to get in his truck, and he fell out and started having convulsions. We washed his face with cold water and revived him. It concerned me so much that I insisted that he go to the doctor. I went with him. The doctor said it was epilepsy. To myself I said, "What? I can't marry this man." I went back to the doctor by myself and asked him about this thing, to ask him how bad it was. I had never really heard about it before. The doctor told me, "Now I gave him some pills. You can feel a spell coming. If he keeps these pills with him all the time, he can take one and hold back the attack. It would give him time if he was driving, to park his car. How often does he have these attacks?"

I said, "I don't know. I'm engaged to marry him, Doctor. I don't really need a burden."

The doctor said he didn't think it would be any problem, because Rice could control it. It probably came from a lick that he had on his head when he was a child. As a matter of fact, I remembered when Rice told me about a time when he and his sister were playing "Heavy, Heavy, Hang Over Your Head," and were throwing rocks over their house, and one hit him in the head.

I went on and married Rice anyhow, but he did have those seizures. He started off having them about every three months after we got married. Mama was crazy about Rice, and said, "What we will do is get down and pray for him." We did, and then the attacks started coming every six months, then once a year, and then they just petered on down until he didn't have them any more.

When we got married, Rice was working at night. My pastor, Reverend Williams, came by Mama's house on his way to his other church on Sunday morning, and married us about nine o'clock. It was in January, in 1953. Mama had breakfast for us all. My niece Helen was staying with Mama, and I wish you could have seen poor Helen. She was the flower girl. I remember I had a lavender dress. We sat down and had breakfast, but Rice was sleepy and tired because he had worked all night. Mama said, "Y'all get on out of here."

I can still see myself and Rice and Miss Lula, walking from Mama's house to his house. It gave me a kind of funny feeling, but that was it. After all those years, that was my husband. Years before, I had gone to a circus and had a fortune-teller woman take my picture and read my hand. She gave a picture of my husband, and it looked just like Rice.

James Myers married again, and I used to see him sometimes, when

I changed buses downtown. He would smile and say hello, and so would I. Marrying him was a bad mistake; it changed my life. But it must have been destined, because otherwise I never would have come to Jacksonville and ended up with all my family around me and married Rice. I feel that somehow it was the divine will of God that brought me out here to this community. I've lived here longer than I have lived any one place in my life.

Marrying Rice was the beginning of a happier and more settled part of my life, a time that I had looked forward to when I was young. If only he could have been my first husband! I am sure that if he had been, I would have gone on with my education and maybe even have gotten a Ph.D. degree. When I married him, he wanted me to go back to school. His cousin was pushing it too; she was commuting to Saint Augustine to Florida Memorial College. I thought over it, and I decided, "All my life I have wanted a husband that I could enjoy and respect and love. I found this. Maybe if I go back to school, I will get a teaching job and be making more money than he does. Maybe I won't respect him as much as I do now. Maybe the reason I had all the trouble with those other two men was that I felt superior to them. I'm contented with things as they are, so why mess it up?" So I didn't go. I told him that I would keep teaching in other ways, in Sunday school and with my nieces and nephews and grandchildren, and wherever I could.

I feel that teaching is an inborn tendency, and I have used it to try to bring peace out of confusion, advising people and counseling young women. Sometimes they call me with terrible problems. I say, as long as he doesn't get a gun after you or injure you so you won't be any good to yourself or anyone else, wait awhile, and see what happens. Usually things work out.

Rice worked at the Railroad Express loading cars, all those years when we were married. He was religious, but not a fanatic, but he loved Sunday school and church. The difference was the denomination. He was a Baptist, but I had been born a Methodist and raised a Methodist. Baptists are more independent than Methodists; they don't have any bishop over them. Each Baptist church is independent unless it joins an association or convention.

Our churches were both close. We would walk a short block to the corner, and he would turn left to go to Mount Bethel Baptist, and I would keep straight on to go to Greggs Temple AME. Our church was still very small. I had tried to get Rice to join my church, because he had been a Methodist at one time. His daddy was Methodist, but his mother was Baptist. But he was satisfied to stay where he was. He never asked me to join his church, but I got to thinking, "Now I sleep with him every night. We are congenial; we really are one. Why can't I worship with him? If I love him enough to marry him, why can't we be in the same church? It's the same Bible, the same God that we are talking about."

I told Mama, and I thought she would be upset, because she was "a Methodist till I die." But she looked at me and said, "Sarah, that is your husband. It would be better if you all were together all the way."

I decided I would go and join him after my church grew a little more, but I didn't tell Rice. My little church needed me until it grew stronger; it wouldn't have been fair to leave them when there were so few members. I loved my little Sunday school class. There was one little old boy in there, smart as a cricket, named Frederick Harper, a good-looking boy. He now has his Ph.D. and has written two books. He's teaching at Howard University. He still remembers me as his Sunday school teacher and says I inspired him. He sent me a book of his poetry.

His mother was never married, and she had three children. When he finished high school, his mother told him, "Now I don't have anything to send you to college with. If you go, you're going to have to go on your own." He got a little secondhand lawnmower and started mowing people's yards that summer. He went to Edward Waters College. He was such a good student that he got a little scholarship, but he still had to work all the way through. When he was president of his class, the board of trustees was going to get rid of the president of the college, but Frederick and the other students fought to keep him and won. After that, he got a scholarship to Howard, and he went on and got his Ph.D. That shows what you can do if you really want to.

When they set Rice up for ordination for a deacon, I went dressed in white to stand with him. It is the custom in the Baptist church for the wife of the man to stand beside him during ordination, and you have to be dressed in white. The ordination comes in the service before they give the invitation for joiners. After they ordained him and gave the invitation for joiners, I don't know what happened, but I just walked up there and joined the church. It hadn't crossed my mind when I left home that morning, but I walked up there and did it. Rice was so happy.

Even though I had been baptized a Methodist, that was only a sprinkling of water. To become a Baptist, I had to be immersed. The next Sunday, I went up to be baptized. The pool was right behind the pulpit, and when I got in that water, I almost drowned that preacher. He was trying to push me down in that water, and I just grabbed him and pulled him down. The chairman of the board of deacons had to jump in there in his suit to save that poor minister.

The first thing they did was put me on the deaconesses' board. These are the women whose husbands are deacons or who are supposed to be sanctified or morally strong. Then I started teaching Sunday school, and before long I was working in the church all over the place.

We have monthly communion at our church. They have a woman they call the mother of the church, who sees after the women. If the women are arguing or fussing, having some kind of disturbance, she's supposed to go and smooth it out. When I joined Mount Bethel, the mother of the church was Mrs. Eliza Henry. The first time I took communion, it was soda crackers. You are supposed to eat unleavened bread with no salt to it. Not only were they saltines, but they had the smell of mothballs, because she kept what was left in her trunk. She was an old lady. I went to the pastor and said, "Reverend, aren't you supposed to have unleavened bread for communion?"

He said, "Yes, ma'am."

I said, "Well, these are saltines that we are having, and they even smell like mothballs."

He said, "Well, that's old Sister Henry, and she's doing the best she can."

I said, "I can make unleavened bread; my mama taught me how to make it. I can make it if you want."

He said, "Well, go ahead."

"No," I said, "I can't do it unless you talk to Sister Henry. I'm not trying to take her job. If she okays it, I'll make it. It's kind of embarrassing; I had some friends come and visit, and they took communion with us. Rice's mama's one of them."

He said, "I'll talk to Sister Henry."

She came to me a couple of weeks later and said, "Reverend Williams said that you can make that communion bread. Child, if you can make it, go ahead and make it. I would sure be glad to get that off my hands." I said I would be glad to, and I have been making it ever since. You take plain flour and pour some water in it. Mix it together, as if you were going to make a batter cake. Stir more flour in until you get it stiff enough to roll. Put in on a board, and roll it as thin as you can get it. Then you put it in a preheated oven at about 250 degrees; it's supposed to kind of dry out. It's just as crisp! I've been doing that for the last thirty years. Now the church has grown big enough so that we could afford to buy it, but the pastor said, "As long as you make it, we'll be glad."

The communion glasses—little teeny individual ones—have to be washed. Sister Henry would take the glasses home and wash them, and sometimes the basket they kept them in would stay back in one of those little old rooms almost two weeks with the glasses in it. I didn't like that, so finally old Mr. Henry went to the pastor before conference and said, "My wife is not doing well. You are going to have to get another church mother, and I suggest Sister Rice for that." A church mother is usually an older woman, but they got up in conference and he made the motion that Sister Rice be church mother. I caught the unreadiness and said, "I'm too young to be a church mother." I was about forty-four then.

The pastor said, "Sister Rice, do you know why they voted for you? They respect you. It's not a matter of age; it's a matter of respect and the confidence the people have in you." He asked me please, and I reluctantly accepted. Then I had to be responsible for the glasses.

The president of the deaconess board would work with the church mother in fixing the communion table. Nobody but she knew anything about how to do that. I went to her and said, "Madam President, I want to give some instruction for the rest of the deaconesses. At one time or another, I might not be here or you might not be here. We could be sick or could be away, and these other deaconesses don't know anything. They need to be trained, and I would like for you and I to give them their instructions." She agreed, and they were so happy to learn how to pour the wine, and how to set up the table.

We used to carry the communion tablecloths from house to house, but some of those people couldn't iron or half wash. I stopped that and said, "These are holy things, and we can't afford to send them to the laundry. We will just let them go to one place, and I'll take care of them." So I still do that.

All this is service that I give to the church. They don't pay me for my starch or my electricity to iron with or my flour for the bread. I give it freely, joyfully. It is really an honor to me to give that kind of service. I taught the women; I showed them how to make the bread. One deaconess, who is dead now, really learned how to make it well. The rest of them are not so sure, but they know how it's made.

CHAPTER EIGHT

Get Up and Live!
(1956–)

G radually I got involved with the local Baptist association and the Women's State Convention. The Emmanuel Progressive Baptist Association is our local group of about twenty-two churches in Jacksonville, banded together for missions and education. It was formed because you can do more for a cause together than you can in driblets. Our pastor is the moderator of it. I decided to go out there and see what the association was all about. When I got there, they were getting ready to have their election of officers for the next year. The women had to make a financial report to the men of fifteen dollars to the parent body. The women were the Women's District Convention Auxiliary, and the men were the parent body. Those women didn't have the fifteen dollars, and they were giving excuses. The moderator said, "I am silencing the women's convention until they are able to make their financial report."

His mother-in-law was the president of the women's convention, and his wife was next door getting the food ready. When that happened, she came up and said, "I'm not speaking as your wife; I'm speaking as a member of the women's convention. I think the women ought to be able to go ahead and hold their election." The moderator said, "Sit down, Sister Williams." Another visitor they had, a state officer, got up and wanted to speak. He said, "Sit down, Sister So-and-So."

I was sitting up there listening and wondering what all this was. I said, "Brother Pastor, may I ask a question, please?"

He said, "Yes, Sister Rice."

I said, "This is an association, is it not?"

He said, "Yes."

I said, "Well, now, the association is just the men? No women are in it at all?"

He said, "Oh, no. Both women and men comprise the association."

I said, "Where do the women get their money to make their reports? Selling fish or sandwiches? Doesn't it come from the churches that they come from? I don't understand. Every church that I go to has more women than men, and the men have made their reports. I can't understand a man not supporting his wife or a pastor not supporting the women of his church. That's all I've got to say. How much are the women supposed to have?"

He said, "Fifteen dollars."

I said, "Well, I'll give something on it."

A preacher jumped up and said, "That sister is right. I feel so ashamed I don't know what to do. Here's five dollars." Then all the preachers got up there and put that money down. I sat back down.

When they got ready to hold the election, I said, "Put me in it as directress of the young people." A young minister got up when the nominating committe brought in the recommendation for officers, and he caught the unreadiness. He said, "I want to offer a substitute motion. The women's convention needs some new blood. I move that that lady over there would be the vice-president." The men all jumped up for me, and the women turned around and looked, wondering who this new person was, coming in there. The president of our deaconess board was the vice-president, but she wasn't there because she had lost her daughter and was in mourning.

I got up and said, "No, I can't take Mrs. Beeman's job."

They said, "She doesn't have a job. All offices are vacant; nobody owns a job in this convention. They are elected by the people annually, and this is the time for elections."

Those women of the church had had it all tied up. Mrs. Williams's mother was the president, and Mrs. Beeman was the vice-president. The women started getting up kind of slowly and frowning; they didn't like the change one cockeyed bit. I came home and told Rice what had happened and said, "When they have their installation, I am going to have a letter of resignation, because those women don't want me for their vice-president."

Rice said, "Leave it alone. You don't know what God has in store for you. It was very unusual for them to get a stranger; those women *fight* over those offices."

So I let it go, and before we had another convention, the president died. In between the conventions, I had to act, because I was the only vice-president. I called all the women together, and nobody came. I called them another time, and one old lady came. I called them the third time, and two came. One told me, "You know why the others haven't come? They're waiting around to see what you are going to do."

I said, "I can't do anything unless I have some officers to do with. I'll tell you what: you go back and tell them that I am going to have a program without them."

The next time I called a meeting, they came. I organized what I called an executive board, and as many women could be a member of it as wanted to. We had meetings monthly. That was twenty-five years ago, and I'm still the president. We still meet monthly, and our convention has grown. We have a dean of religious education, we have study periods, we have programs. We just recently had our twelfth international affair at our convention, where we have twenty countries represented, one for each of the churches in our association. They have a table decorated for every country, and food for each one. Every church marches, and the pastor leads the parade while the people wear the costume of the country they represent. After they march around and sing a song, the food is served. They march around from table to table, and everybody eats as much as they want. Three prizes are given for the best table and food. That's how we raise our educational money to carry to the state convention which meets in April.

Every now and then, some of the narrow Baptists would say about me, "She came from the Methodist church," as if I were an intruder. They said I had Methodist ideas; well, whatever the ideas were, they were succeeding. Somebody asked them why they were worrying about it, since we were progressing. That shut that one off.

The proportion of men to women in the church is roughly one-fourth men, *if* they all come. But when I was growing up in Alabama, most black folks went to church; that was the only place they had as an organization. Even though most of the members now are women, the men run the show. The women's groups are always auxiliaries; they can't make any rules unless the men say they can. The minister will tell you quickly that he is in power and that God gave him directions to tell you what to do. Some of them give you to believe that the Holy Spirit doesn't talk to anybody but the preacher. But when they want something done, a financial effort, money raised or given, it is more or less the women who do it. From the biblical days on down, from the women who followed Jesus, it was the women who were giving service. I guess it always will be that way. Now that people are more affluent and have other interests scattered all about, they don't go to church much, especially the men. But now in the Baptist church, the women are getting in the ministry. The men are giving them a hard time. I have a little friend in Tallahassee whose husband was a minister, and she told him that God had called her. She had her master's degree a long time ago and was teaching. He said, "God hasn't called any woman. You'll never preach in my church."

She had a sister who lived in New York, who she visited quite often. This sister was a Baptist minister, and her pastor let her help him. So my friend went to New York and got her sister's pastor to ordain her. Her husband was much older than she was, and he got sick after she went back home, and so he had to let her keep the church going. He died, and the members of that church called her. She is the secretary of the Ministerial Alliance up there, and she has been carrying truckloads of things to help the people in poverty up somewhere in Mississippi. Agencies in Tallahassee give her stuff that she takes.

In our national convention, they have a Tuesday night for the women ministers, and these beautiful women ministers have such eloquence! I just looked at them. One of them was married to a minister, and her husband said that all the people God called were men, so she bided her time, and he got sick. The congregation had to call different ministers in to preach for him. They had to pay each one of these, but their sick minister was still getting his regular salary. It was such a strain on the membership, that he called the deacons and said, "I know it's hard on the church, but I do need my salary. My wife said God called her. Of course I don't necessarily go along with women preaching, but if I ordain her, will you all let her carry on until I get better or deceased?" They said yes; they loved him. They ordained her, and she carried on the church. He died, and they called her to pastor. But then the state and the national conventions dropped her church, because they didn't want a woman pastor. She didn't cry; she went out in the community and organized agencies to help the underprivileged and to feed the people. The church grew by leaps and bounds, as she ministered to the people, witnessing and giving and sharing and loving them all. They had to expand the church. Her name is Trudy Trim. Then the state and national bodies were glad to have her back.

In our convention, we have a woman named Hester Ross, a big, stout, robust woman. They won't even call her Reverend Ross; they call her Mother Ross. One time at the convention, she said, "My members told me not to bring any money to this convention if I wasn't recognized as a minister." Then they gave her the recognition. It looks like we just have to fight for what we want. We are supposed to be one, and walking side by side, but they don't see it that way. But I think we are making pretty good strides. Some of us are getting it kind of wrong; there are more ways to catch a fly than swat him. You can be sweet and get much more than you can by being bitter.

The Baptists support Florida Memorial College. It was at Saint Augustine, but it is down in Miami now and growing by leaps and bounds. It almost closed two or three times. Our president of the Florida General Baptist Women's Convention, Mrs. Susie B. Harley, one of the greatest women, saved that college.

I first became involved with her at the first state convention I went to. She was elected president, and there was one woman in the convention, a Mrs. Parker, that thought she should have been president. She was experienced and learned, but she was a controversial person, real mean and hard to get along with. When she lost out to Mrs. Harley, she would always try to put little sneaky, conniving, little trap things in the way.

The first time I went, I only stayed one day, because I didn't have the money to properly represent our church. Nobody had told me about that. But the next year, I was the elected president and had my representation. The meeting was in Tallahassee, and they were revising their constitution. Mrs. Parker was the chairman of that committee, and she was the president of the biggest association women's convention in the state. They had passed out copies of the present constitution and copies of the proposed constitution. We were supposed to study it and vote on it the next day.

I used to make my own hats, and make them kind of flamboyant. The next day, I was sitting in the audience. Nobody knew me but the folks from Jacksonville. I caught the unreadiness. Mrs. Parker got up and read the proposed constitution, and somebody jumped up and offered a motion that we receive it and adopt it. Somebody seconded the motion, but I caught the unreadiness and raised my hand. But nobody caught the unreadiness of Sister A. O. Parker; *nobody* challenged that woman. She looked around as if to say, "What little upstart is challenging me?"

Mrs. Harley, our president, said, "The sister with the pretty hat on, will you stand?" That was me.

I said, "My unreadiness is, that article so-and-so in the original constitution said that the president would appoint all committees and committee chairmen. Article so-and-so in the proposed constitution says the committees are supposed to be elected by the body. That would take away the powers of the president. I think all presidents should be able to appoint committees; therefore I offer a substitute motion that that article would be deleted from the proposed constitution."

Mrs. Harley started smiling, and my motion passed. Old Sister Parker came back to me and said, "Who are you?"

I said, "I'm Sarah Rice."

She said, "Hmm. You are all right, I guess."

When we broke for lunch, Mrs. Harley called me over and said she wanted to talk to me. She said, "I'm putting you on the education committee."

When I got to the room where the committee was meeting, the

chairman of the committee was from Saint Augustine, a tiny little woman, well educated and a doctor's widow. She said, "Who are you?"

I said, "I am Mrs. Sarah L. Rice from Jacksonville, the president of the Emmanuel Progressive Woman's District Convention."

"Oh, yes," she said, "You're the one who made the substitute motion." Everyone said, "Oh yes."

I said, "I was sent here by President Harley to work on the committee."

She said, "Well, I've already filled the positions on the committee." Two of the former members had passed away.

I said, "Well, good. I'll go tell Mrs. Harley that you used your authority to appoint members of the committee. That's just what we got through voting on. That's nice." I was just smiling, not acting like I was mad or anything.

"Oh, wait a minute! Wait a minute!" she said.

Two of those committee members she had couldn't count. Now all the money comes in from the district, for education, that's going to be turned over to the schools. That committee has to count it and turn it over to the finance committee, and get receipts for it. That's the system of checks and balances. You have to write down the associations that the money's coming from, how much each church contributes. Everything has to balance. The finance committee chairman told me later that the education committee always had trouble balancing the figures. The total was always off, usually a little less than what they said it was.

The chairman of the education committee asked me if I could count, and I said, "I can count all the money that this convention is going to receive this year, and all the money that the men are going to take in too."

She said, "Well, all right then."

She sat down with a pad of paper and started making a receipt. I said, "Do you mean to tell me that the convention can't get a receipt book?" Anybody could bring money to this convention and write out a receipt and carry it back to their churches and say they paid it, when they didn't. I said I would go get one, and I did. Then she counted the money and turned it over to me, but she had lost three hundred dollars overnight. She said she put it in a magazine. I said, "We should have all our money in, before the finance committee closes down. Don't carry any money home with you." From then on, she would count the money and hand it over to me, I would count it to verify it, and I would carry it to the finance committee. It never got lost again. She got sick, and her daughter came down from New York City and got her. She wrote a letter to Mrs. Harley, recommending me as chairman for that education committee because she didn't think she would be able to come back to Florida. I've been chairman ever since. Mrs. Harley nicknamed me Glamour, because I expressed myself, I guess.

Mrs. Harley used to teach at Florida Memorial College, and her husband was the president of the college for a time. It had started in Live Oak, Florida, from money the old folks had saved up in snuff boxes, and then they had put it together with a little independent Baptist school in Jacksonville and moved it to Saint Augustine to create Florida Memorial College. She would ride all over Florida in an old T-model Ford with about five or six hooters and sing in churches. They would get syrup, and meat, and whatever they had to offer and pick up pennies in these snuff boxes these sisters had saved for the school. She said that sometimes they wouldn't have enough to pay her own and her husband's salaries, but they would pay the other teachers' salaries. They were living on the school grounds, and at least they would have something to eat. They were dedicated.

Florida Memorial College really started going down the totem pole during the late 1960s, early 1970s. It was during the time of the civil rights marches, and some of the students had gotten involved in it. The city of Saint Augustine used to give the students jobs. When all this happened, the city stopped and wouldn't give a black student a job, even if he would do it for only twenty cents. The city also cut out giving support to the college itself. It got to the point where there wasn't enough money in the bank to support the teachers' salaries or the regular maintenance of the school. The men were all ready to give up the school; the preachers were saying, "There's no reason to support that school; we have lost it." But Mrs. Harley said no. It was too important to give up.

Mrs. Harley started what she called Donation Day. We would carry down once a year, during November, a dollar off our Thanksgiving dinner, and carry down rice and peas and other foodstuffs down to the school in truckloads from all over the state. Then they turned the feeding over to a private concern, so we started to carry dollars.

Later on, Mrs. Harley asked us to sell dinners. In every church, the women get together and sell dinners and make their money and send it to the school. This started in the late 1960s. After that, she asked us to take a dollar off our Sunday dinners; if we were going to buy a roast, use beans instead or a neck bone.

I had a dream, that some white man was going to come to the school and was going to save us. I saw it just as clear as day, and I thought we were rejoicing. I told the women in our state workshop about this dream, and I said, "This dream is so realistic, until it is going to happen." Everybody looked at me, some of them kind of sly, and said, "Fortune-teller Rice." At our next Donation Day, not very long after that, when we went down to Saint Augustine, we got ready to give our reports, and this white man came forth. I can't remember now where he was from, but he was not from Florida. He had been approached, and he gave so many thousand dollars to that school, that brought us over the hump. I stood up in the meeting and said, "Praise the Lord!" I started walking up and down the aisles, and others started following me. I said, "I know the Lord will provide." Everybody remembered Sarah's dream.

The preachers started believing that God was going to let us keep the school, and then they came back in line. The president of the college said that if the college moved down to the Miami area, where there is a lot of business and a lot of wealth, it might be able to make it. To make the move, they bought some land down near Hollywood, Florida, and built our present campus. It is beautiful. The president of the college is Willie C. Robinson, a North Carolinian, and he is *something*! Now the students are able to get work, and we have students from the

Bahamas and Haiti and Liberia, as well as from Florida and other parts of the South.

When Mrs. Harley would be in Jacksonville on convention business, she would come to our house. There was another lady who wanted power and recognition. She said to Mrs. Harley, "Now, I have prepared a room for you when you come to town." It was pretty, all fixed up nice. But she would always come to my house and go back in that hole, that little extra bedroom of ours. She would say, "You and Deacon Rice just make me feel at home." She traveled a lot, riding the buses, and her ankles would swell. When she was sick, she would still go. So when she came to our house, she would flop down on the bed, and I would get the foot tub and some hot water and Epsom salts and soak her feet and rub them down. She liked coffee the way I do, and we'd sit up drinking coffee and talking into the night about the women's association business. I knew all the plans about the convention. She would tell me the things she wanted to do, and the programs she wanted to put on, and when she would bring it out in our board meeting, I knew exactly what she was talking about, and I would get up and make the motion.

We were very close. Whenever I went to a meeting, no matter where it was, she would ask, "Sister Rice, how are you doing?"

I would say, "I'm doing all right."

She would ask, "Do you have enough to make it?"

I would say, "I think so." It was so expensive eating in restaurants at those conventions that I couldn't be spending all that money for food. So I would always carry sardines and crackers. I would get one hot meal a day. For the rest of it, I had my little coffeepot, and I carried some cereal and some powdered milk. I would eat some cereal and drink coffee for my breakfast. For lunch, I would wait until way over in the day, and then I would eat a hot meal. At night when I came home, I heated water in my coffeepot and had some dried soup and crackers.

I even had some guests, and Mrs. Harley was one of them. One night she said, "I don't feel like going downtown to eat." I told her what I had, so she said, "Okay, let's go up to your room." We had sardine sandwiches and hot soup.

Her second vice-president passed, and she said, "Sister Rice, I'm going to recommend you."

I said, "Oh no. Several other women in that convention would be good for you."

She said, "I know what would be good for me." She was a woman to talk straight down to the ground. She didn't put on anything. She told me to keep that to myself.

I thanked her for believing I was worthy of being her second vice-president and said I didn't want to be a hindrance to her and that if I couldn't be an asset, I would just rather back off. She said, "You could become the president of this women's convention. You have the know-how, the charisma, and everything, and the Holy Spirit certainly guides you."

Sure enough, I was elected second vice-president. A friend of mine from Hollywood, Florida, worked in a craft department, and she would always bring me something she had made, to the convention. When I was elected, she said, "Now that you are second vice-president, I suppose you are going to look over me."

I said, "You really don't know me well, do you? I'm going to love you more than ever, because I am going to need you. Before, we just supported each other. Now I need your total support and your prayers. I am treading in deep water, and I could drown."

By now, I am the first vice-president. Mrs. Harley passed between two conventions, so the first vice-president had to make all the pro forma arrangements for our women's convention and preside during that time until an election was held.

Both Rice and I kept very busy with our church work and with our jobs through the 1950s and 1960s. He worked for the railroad all those years, for Railway Express. I stopped work for a year or so in 1956. My mother had passed in 1955, and not long after that, Miss Lula got real sick. She was about ninety-one years old. I quit all the jobs I had, and stayed home and took care of her. I had made that promise to her, that if I was physically able, she would never have to go into a nursing home. She had a horror of going into a nursing home. Everybody thought I was foolish to stay home with her and nurse her, when she wasn't related to me at all. But I did; I took care of her and kept her clean. Even at the last, when the doctor told me she was dying of old age, I asked him if he could give me some light water. She had stopped eating. He asked me why. I said, "I want to be sure that I've done all I could to keep her living."

He said, "Okay, if that's what you want." So he came in and set up an IV for her. About one-third of that IV was used before she went. I felt good, because I knew that I had done the best I could. I couldn't have done any more for Mama, and in fact, I did more for Miss Lula than I did for Mama.

I decided to go back to work, but the Thompsons had moved to Tampa by then. I had a friend, who was also a member of my church, that I had helped to get a job. The people that she was working for had a friend by the name of Mrs. Louise Hutchings, who was looking for some help. She asked this friend of mine if she knew anybody, and my friend got in touch with me and told me about this lady who seemed like a nice person and needed some help. I thought I would give it a try. So in March of 1956, I started work at Mrs. Hutchings's house in Southside, on Saratoga Road. I knew as soon as I met her that we were going to make it. She was very nice and just accepted me like she knew me all along. She had a baby and three older children, two girls in junior high school and a boy about ten. I never could get used to that house, because it was dark inside and on a wet piece of ground. The flowers just bloomed in profusion, but it would flood when it rained a lot, and things would get damp and musty. They were building a new house, though, about five miles farther out in the south part of town, and they moved out there not long after I came to work for them. It was a much bigger house with plenty of light and on a high piece of ground.

I only worked for Mrs. Hutchings one day a week, and then I worked for the Hirshbergs the rest of the time. And when the Hirshbergs moved to Tampa, I started working for some people named Davis. All those were nice people, and they all lived on the Southside of Jacksonville.

Things were going well for Rice and me until the 1970s, when we started having some health problems. Lib and Rice and I were on our way to Eufala to the funeral of my niece's mother-in-law one time in about 1973, in Rice's old piece of Buick. It was cold weather, and the car windows were rolled up. Rice had run over a railroad track and knocked the exhaust pipe off, and there was a hole in the back part of the floor of the car. Nobody paid any attention to it. I had done a lot of work and was tired, so I decided to get in the back seat and sleep. When we got to Sanford, we were talking, but then they heard a strange snoring sound from the back. Lib called me, because I don't usually snore, and I didn't answer. She looked back there and I was out.

She said, "Rice, stop this car! There's something wrong with Sarah!" He got to a place where he could pull off, and they stopped. I had on a beautiful yellow wool coat that Mrs. Davis had given me, and some kind of black stuff had run out of my mouth on the coat. I never could get that stuff out of that coat. Rice and Lib couldn't revive me, so Rice turned around and Lib said, "Go, go!" and got back in the back seat with me, holding me in her lap.

When Rice got to Saint Luke's Hospital, Lib was out too. Rice jumped out and hollered, "Come get my wife!! My wife!" The guy pulled Lib out first, because she was on his side. Rice hollered, "That isn't my wife!" They treated Lib and she revived quickly, but they carried me upstairs. I didn't know anything. When I woke up, I was in a private room, and my daughter-in-law was sitting there in a chair. It was at night. Everybody had said I was dead. They even called President Harley and told her. My poor little old pastor was running around praying and going on.

I had had a dream, that I had walked out, kind of floated out, on this precipice on a high mountaintop, and I could look deep down in the valley. It was all lit up with all kinds of beautiful lights. It looked like foam or soapsuds, the way it does when you ride in a plane sometimes and look down. Just as pretty as you have ever seen.

I wanted to step out, off that precipice, and I felt as though I would just float down into the valley, but just as I was about to step off, a hand grabbed me and pulled me back. A voice said, "Not now."

When I woke up and saw darkness, I said to my daughter-in-law, "What am I doing here?"

She said, "Mama Sarah, we thought we were going to lose you."

Rice had a similar kind of dream one time when he was sick. He dreamed that he was sick or dying or had died. He said, "Well, I don't have anybody left that loves me or cares for me, so it's okay to die." He was walking in the light, and the house all of a sudden, rose right up before him with the legs or foundation pillars hanging on to it. I came walking under the house and said, "You've got me." He was so relieved.

Rice hadn't had any epileptic trouble or any other problems with his health for years. The first real sickness he had was in 1977, and that was prostate trouble. One night it was raining, just *raining!* Rice went to the bathroom and came back and said, "I am about to die, take me to the hospital!" I knew something was wrong, because he never said things like that. I was just learning to drive, and it was raining so hard the windshield wipers would hardly let you see. But I got in the car with Rice and said a little prayer and took him to Saint Luke's. I didn't want to go to University because sometimes they make you wait so long. At Saint Luke's they took him right in, and Dr. Jones, a urologist, came through while they were working on Rice, and he helped them to get the water coming. Dr. Jones suggested moving Rice to University, so that it would be less expensive for us, and he said he would still see about him. So he moved and stayed there about a week. Then he came home and later had to go back for an operation. When he was in the hospital, he wanted me there every day, and I went.

When we were leaving the hospital, I was worried about paying what is left over after the insurance has paid. I thought I might have to borrow some money or either have my brother cosign a note, or something. But friends and people from the church had been coming to see Rice in the hospital and giving him money to help out. I had saved all that. When we went by the office to check out, it turned out that I had enough to pay all but about fifty dollars!

After that operation, Rice seemed to be weaker; he just never got back his full strength, and he gradually declined. A year or two later, we were leaving church one time when it was hot weather, and he just fell out, unconscious. We rushed him to the hospital, and the doctor said he didn't think he was going to live. He had had a stroke and was comatose. He came out of that, and he went to the rehab place and stayed there awhile. He wanted to see me every day, and I was there every day, going in the morning and staying until it got dark. The people at the hospital and at the rehab center said that they had never seen anybody so attentive as I was to him.

When we brought him home from the rehab center, we got on the expressway, and he just broke down and cried, he was so happy. After that he had two or three years before he got sick again, and they were good years. He was one of the trustees, as well as a deacon of the church. He kept up with the money. I tried to keep him out of that office, because that kind of work was frustrating, but I couldn't keep him out.

Between the times of his sickness, Rice would always jump back. One morning his sister didn't go to work, and her boss lady called me and asked me where she was. I said, "Well, I suppose she has gone to work."

The lady said, "It's ten o'clock, and she hasn't got here yet."

I said, "Well, maybe the bus broke down or something like that, because she is a dependable person. I'll go over to the house and check."

I went over and called her, but she didn't answer. The shades were still down, which was strange, because she would always raise the shades in the morning when she got up. I went around to the front, where her bedroom was. The shade was up just a few inches, and I could stand on the ground and look in. There she was, stretched out on the bed on top of the cover. This was during the fall of the year, and it was cold. I knocked on the window, beat on that window, but she didn't move. I had a key, so I came over to my house and got it and went back and went in. She wasn't dead, but she was comatose.

Rice was gone somewhere, so I called the ambulance. They took her to the hospital, and she was there two weeks. She never regained consciousness, and she passed.

Rice's nephews had died, and all he had left was a grandnephew and some cousins, but they were distant. He and I got closer and closer, and Rice looked so robust and was doing fine. One morning he sat at the table and got up to ask the blessing for our breakfast.

It had been my birthday the day before, and Rice had carried me out to dinner. He had asked me where I would like to go, and I had said Sister's, a fish place. He took me and Lib and his cousin Grace. We all had birthdays within a few months of each other. Rice had stopped driving by this time, because the doctor didn't want him to do any more. So I went up and picked up Lib and Grace, and we went to Sister's. We had been to Sister's many times, but he had never ordered all oysters. This time he did, and his cousin kind of teased him about it and said, "Aw, you're trying to get to be a man again." He slightly smiled, but he didn't talk much, and he didn't eat all his oysters. He got up and went to the bathroom, and then Lib went to the bathroom too. He couldn't find his way out, so Lib helped him. He was quiet all the way home.

After he had been sick, I started sleeping in a different bedroom with the wide bed where I could stretch my legs out. Rice stayed in the other room with twin beds, and when he was sick, I would stay in there with him in the other bed.

He got up that morning. I had brought back a doggie bag from the restaurant, because I couldn't eat all on my platter. I heated that up for our breakfast, and made a pot of grits. Rice got up to ask the blessing, and said, "Spshwsh wshwhish . . ." He couldn't get the words out. A pang went through me, but I wasn't thinking about the bad part. I looked up and said, "Are you praying?" He said something else, and I knew something was happening, but I wasn't going to say anything and was hoping maybe he would come back to himself.

He finished his breakfast and stood up and backed himself up against the heater. I said, "Rice, you don't look like you feel so good. Do you feel all right?" He shook his head. I said, "Why don't you go back and lie back down. Maybe you will feel better." He turned around and went back into his room. I followed him in there, and he pulled off his pants and shoes, but not his shirt. He got in the bed and kind of curled up like an S. I pulled the cover up over him and said, "Well, I'll go out and wash out a few things."

I had started the water when Lib walked up. I told her, "There is something wrong with Rice. Go in there and check on him, and see what you think." She went in, and then she came tearing back out, saying, "Rice is comatose! Rice is comatose!" I said, "He couldn't be! It hasn't been ten minutes!"

We called the ambulance and they carried him to the hospital, and they worked over him. Rice's doctor, Dr. Lee, met us there at the emergency room. They ran me out of the way, because I was just about nuts. He never came to, and they put him on that old pumping thing. We had talked about that before, and he didn't want it. They were just blowing him up, just blowing air in him. He puffed all up. I told Dr. Lee that he had decided he didn't want that, if he was brain dead. I said, "If God is ready to let him live on his own, let him live, but I can't stand to go in there and see him with all those machines on him."

Dr. Lee was so good to Rice. He was there all the time with him. One night he stayed nearly all night. He understood our wish, and he took him off those machines, and God freed Rice from that misery. He died on January 7, 1983.

My family gathered around me and supported me when Rice passed. James David and my brother J.D. and my sister Lib, my niece Helen here, and my niece Elizabeth from Geneva, Alabama, were all with me. I sat in my chair, and friends and acquaintances and men from Rice's lodge would come to the house offering sympathy. I have a little footstool, and they would come and sit on the footstool and console me. "Oh, Sister Rice, I'm so sorry. The Lord said such and such and such. How did it happen? Were you there when he passed?" I would answer and cry a little. That one would get up, and the time he would get up from the stool, another one would sit right down. Same thing over and over.

Lib just got sick of it all and said, "Sarah, get up and go in the room and get in the bed." It was just killing me, but their intentions were good, and I didn't want to make anybody feel bad. That door stayed open all day long and into the night. Lib and Helen and Elizabeth tried to protect me, but some just demanded to see me anyway.

Finally it came time for the funeral. All my family came from everywhere. Rice loved his Masonic Lodge. All the members came in their uniforms. The church was packed with people, along with the people I had worked for. It was such a rewarding thing to look up and see Mrs. Hutchings, Mrs. Davis, and some others. During the service the pastor was pretty full too, because Rice had helped so much with the building of the church. He had given so much service to the church. He could do most anything; he could take a saw and a hammer and a nail and really do wonderful things. By him being one of the deacons and a trustee of the church, he had a lot to do with the hiring and firing of the builders who were working on the church.

After the funeral, we came home, and all my family left to go back home. I was so sad or so upset or something, until I started feeling heavyhearted. It was a heavy feeling in the chest. Lib and the rest of them insisted that I go to the doctor. I went to Dr. Lee, who gave me a thorough examination and found out that something was wrong with a blood vessel running to the heart. I thought about my father, who had a bad heart, and I thought it was something I had inherited. It seemed to me that I was going behind Rice, that I was going to die pretty soon too. I was just giving up. I was thinking about making a last will and testament; I wanted to be sure that my son would get my little house, because that's all I had. I had enough insurance, I thought, to bury me. I was talking to Helen about it, and she said, "Aunt Sarah, shut up. Nothing is going to happen to you. Stop talking about dying."

Every morning I would wake up and say, "Oh, I'm still here. Thank you, Lord!" I would look around, and I could *see*. When I would get up and hit the floor, I was so happy, I didn't know what to do. One day I was sitting up in my chair and went off into a nap, and a voice came to me, saying, "Get up and live!" I decided that I was going to die anyhow one day, whenever God got ready for me, and I was going to do all the good I could for the rest of my time. Ever since that time, I haven't feared death. I had feared it up until then. I have the feeling that one day I will go to sleep, and I just won't wake up. From then on, I redoubled my efforts and my work. I went back to my old profession of teaching younger women the things I have learned, and I went back fully into my work at our church, Mount Bethel Missionary Baptist Church, where I am church mother and president of the Deaconess Board Number 1. I picked up work again with our Women's District Convention Auxiliary Number 2 and my job as first vice-president of the Women's State Convention.

My family kept me from feeling lonesome. Lib and J.D. and James David were right around me in my neighborhood. James David was in his early forties when he retired. Then he got a job driving a city bus and did that for a while, and then finally he retired from that. Now he is just working in his garden and around his house. Boy, that guy can grow stuff; he can just touch stuff and it grows. He has got OKRA, going to bed! So he's doing all right.

James David's son Willie Fred was an Eagle Scout, and then he went off to the Vietnam War and came back a changed man. He was really deflated by that war. But he married a nurse who is a lovely person, and they have two children, a son named Willie Charles, and a daughter named Katrina. James David's daughter Lisa is going to Florida Junior College.

Through the years, we kept in touch with other parts of the family, like Beatrice's family in Alabama and my brother James's family in Tennessee. We also had found some of our Webb relatives in Georgia and had reunions with them.

After Rice and I had been married quite a while, I had gone to Eufala to visit my niece, and I went with Helen. (Her name was Mary Helen, and she was my baby sister Catherine's daughter, who we all raised together.) Before we left Eufala, we were talking about relatives we had in Cedar Springs, Georgia. I said, "It's a funny thing, as many Georgia people as I know, and I know quite a few, none that I have talked with knew anything or had even heard of a place in Georgia called Cedar Springs."

My brother-in-law spoke up and said, "It's not that far from here. People from Eufala carry logs down there." It was just across the state line. He said it would be about seventy-five miles out of the way back home to Jacksonville. I thought it would be worth it to try.

Helen had a station wagon, and her oldest boy was with us. We drove to Blakely, Georgia, and Cedar Springs was out from there. We found the road and got on it, and after we had gotten out so far, we saw a farmhouse that was sitting right out on the roadside, a little elevated on a clean-swept red yard. It had a porch clean across it. I told Helen, "Stop here and ask this lady if she knows anything about Cedar Springs. We can't be far from it, and people will remember an old family like ours."

Sure enough, that lady knew. She said, "You go right up the road there, and the first road to the left, you turn left and go back up the road."

A long time before, we had met some of our cousins on Mama's side. This time we were looking for relatives from Papa's side. When we got to the door, a man came to the door and inquired about what we wanted. We asked for Fanny Powell, and the man said, "Oh yes, she lives here," and she came to the door. I said, "I'm your cousin."

She said, "My what?"

I said, "Did you have an uncle you called Jimmy?"

She said, "Yes."

I said, "Well, I'm Uncle Jimmy's daughter Sarah."

She said, "Oh, Lord have mercy!" and opened the door, and we went in, and she just hugged us and said, "We wondered where you all were, and we tried to find out something after Uncle Jimmy died. Aunt Lizzie came to see us and brought some little children, and we heard that she had gotten married, but we didn't know who she got married to. So we couldn't find out anything, and we never heard from her any more after that."

She carried me in the house and named all of her sisters and brothers that were still living. One was named Charlotte Robinson, who lived in Gainesville, Florida. The other daughter lived in Lake Butler, Florida. Her name was Charity Moore. When she said, "Charity," that rang a bell, because Beatrice's name was Charity Beatrice Webb. She was named for Papa's mama, and so was this cousin Charity. Another sister was Ellen Pridgins, who lived in Perry, Florida. And there was one brother, John Wiley Webb, who lived in Rivera Beach, Florida. Another sister's name was Charlie May Harris, who lived in Thomasville, Georgia. Another sister's name was Julia Smith, and she lived in Blakeley, Georgia. We got the addresses of all of them, and I wrote all of them a letter and got a quick response.

We were still in Blakeley, Georgia, and this Fanny Powell was living about a third of a block from where she was born. The chimney of the old house was still there.

Uncle John was a schoolteacher. His baby brother couldn't read, but he scuffled and got himself an education. If you were smart and were a good sixth-grade student, you could teach what they were getting in the country. School out there didn't last more than about three months, anyway. So Uncle John taught school and farmed. Since he had the farm, the girls had to do the plowing, because the one boy was way down the line. Charity said he was strict on them, but he believed in education. So they all learned how to read and write, and they grew up to be progressive-minded people. Some of them are teachers and some are still farming, and they have children who are active in their communities. Among the children is an accomplished musician, and many who have college educations.

We have been having family reunions for years, but before we met these cousins, it was just Beatrice and all her children, and Mama's side of the family. But once we met these Webb cousins, they started to come too. In 1985 we had a huge one. I had cooked up cakes, cakes, cakes, cakes, going to bed! I must have had about ten or fifteen cakes, had them stuck all about. Lib helped me too, because she makes good pound cakes. I made the coconuts and the chocolates and the jelly cake. They went right through them. We went to the place where they sell day-old bread, and had plenty of bread.

The first morning, a Saturday, breakfast was at my house. All of them that weren't too tired from their trips came to my house. We scrambled eggs, we had pots of grits, and they came in and served themselves. The ones that were too tired stayed in the hotel.

After that, we went over to the church to get acquainted. From there, they went to the beach in a bus we had rented. When they came back from the beach, we had the barbeque here in our neighborhood. People were just dragging from one house to another, visiting with everybody and eating.

The next day, Sunday morning, we had full charge of the morning worship at our church. We had a choir made up of our family, with Helen playing the piano and her son Junior playing the organ. They both can sing, and Elizabeth has a beautiful voice. They all sang up a storm. Albert, Beatrice's son who is a minister in California, brought the message. We took a special family offering and turned it over to the church. They had the regular public offering, and then we had a special table to put our offering on. It was really beautiful.

After the service, we had Sunday dinner in the church dining room. All the family got in there. We had our family tree up on display—we got an old dead tree and had ribbons of different colors for the different branches of the family, and they were hanging on the tree with everybody's names on them. I had baked a turkey, Lib cooked a ham, we had fried chicken, dressing, collard greens, peas, okra. We all just walked around and stuffed. Then Lib said, "Those of you who are going to get in the car and start traveling, fix you a lunch." So they went around the leftovers and made lunches. Some of them left that Sunday evening, and some stayed over until Monday, and some stayed over until Tuesday. It was really exciting, and I just wish Beatrice could have been living, because Beatrice just loved kinfolks. She would have loved to meet these relatives of ours. They were so wonderful and so much like us, progressive-minded people, so some of that must have come from Papa's side, as well as from my mama. Just to think that from my grandfather not being able to read or write, or his wife either, and coming up from slavery, all this family grew. When the slaves were freed, they didn't have any direction or anybody to tell them what to do, so they were almost as bad off as during slavery. But now, here we all were together, all these branches of the family, including teachers and nurses and preachers and businessmen and musicians. Wouldn't Mama and Papa have been proud?

Through all the trials and tribulations I've had, I'm still reminded of Mama's old song, "He Included Me," and I know it's true, because otherwise I wouldn't be here to tell this story. "When the Lord said, 'Whosoever will,' He included me too." Yes, Jesus included me. Yes, Jesus included me.